D0045590

On the Triangle Run

On the Triangle Run

James B. Lamb

Macmillan of Canada
A Division of Canada Publishing Corporation
Toronto, Ontario, Canada

First Printing, August, 1986
Second Printing, September, 1986
Third Printing, October, 1986

Canadian Cataloguing in Publication Data

Lamb, James B., date.
On the triangle run

Bibliography: p.
ISBN 0-7715-9746-0

1. World War, 1939-1945 — Naval operations, Canadian.
2. World War, 1939-1945 — Atlantic Ocean. I. Title.

D779.C3L35 1986 940.54'5971 C86-093854-9

Edited by Maggie MacDonald
Designed by Don Fernley

Macmillan of Canada
A Division of Canada Publishing Corporation
Printed in Canada

CONTENTS

To
C.P.O. Harold Schmeisser,
our indomitable coxswain,
this book is
respectfully dedicated.

FOREWORD

IT IS the stuff of nightmares.

At half past two in the morning, during our watch below, they tumble us out; every upper-deck seaman is needed aft for some emergency. We peer blearily from our swaying hammocks at a world gone mad, a world lit only by dim blue lights and filled with the tremendous noise and violence of the hurricane outside. We step out in our stocking feet into the six inches of cold salt water that has flooded in over the fo'c'sle-door coaming, are hurled against a stanchion as the ship crashes down into the trough, then clutch at our hammocks for support as our whole world suddenly rushes upward, borne by a mountainous sea. The insensate din, the motion, the rushing water overwhelm the senses: we push our sodden feet into our seaboots and shrug into our cowled duffle coats in a kind of numbed stupor before groping towards the door to the well-deck, pushing off the dog-clips that hold it shut, and peering out at the terrible scene outside.

Our little corvette is staggering to windward into a maelstrom of roaring, breaking water and flying spray, rolling her waist-decks under: the shrieking of the wind numbs the mind, the tumult of the driven sea fills the black void all about us. One by one we catch hold of the taut lifeline with both hands and fight our way aft down the port side as the ship rolls to starboard. Before we are halfway along, the ship rolls back to port, and we hold on for dear life as the furious sea thunders in over the bulwark, soaking us to the armpits and threatening to carry us off with it into the blackness beyond. As the water recedes, we stumble on to reach the relative security of the quarterdeck, and join the knot of shadowy figures huddled there in the lee of the minesweeping winch.

The coxswain is here, a burly, compact figure in his duffle coat and oilskins, his face a blur of white as he shouts his orders in our ears. At his urging we climb down the greasy ladder into the tiller-flat, clammy with steam from the clattering steering engine, and set about rousing out the towing hawser, an enormously long and heavy nylon rope, thick as a man's thigh, with pennants of strong steel wire spliced into each end. Others are hauling up the rest of the gear needed to tow — monstrous snatch-blocks and huge steel shackles — for the first lieutenant, peering down through the hatch above, tells us that we are going to try to put a line aboard a ten-thousand-ton merchant ship that has lost her propeller. Riding light in ballast, she is unmanageable in this hurricane and may well roll herself under and be overwhelmed unless we can pull her head around into the seas.

Fear is at our elbow through all the crowded hours that follow. Fear of the frightful cliff of rusting, barnacled steel that towers up over us as the captain takes us right down alongside the stricken vessel, now plunging and rolling and lashing out like a fear-maddened elephant, in the grasp of the terrible seas. Fear as our own little ship, slowed almost to a standstill to pass a line across, is suddenly caught by a gigantic wave and dashed sideways under that immense, up-rearing bow. Fear as the huge merchantman, feeling for the first time the tentative restraint of the new-passed tow, sheers violently to one side, lifting our spouting, tautened hawser clear of the sea and pulling us bodily sideways into the trough, where the enormous oncoming wave rolls us almost under. Fear as a deck fitting carries away, letting a wire of the relieving tackle tauten to snapping-point. In a second it will break like a piece of spaghetti; anyone caught near its whipping, vicious end could be cut in half. We stand appalled — but one of us, braving the risk, leaps to the bollard and renders slack to the tortured wire, easing its intolerable strain — and we learn to venerate courage.

We learn much that night: to respect the sea-sense of our captain, grey-faced and grim on the distant bridge, and the calm competence of the coxswain directing our efforts. Above all, in the teeth of that elemental enemy, the sea, all of us, still only a few months removed from the sunlit serenity of classroom or the tree-lined back streets of some inland Canadian town, are made aware that here the petty distinctions of the shore count for nothing. On this spray-swept quarterdeck it does not matter whether your parents are rich or poor, whether you went to university or flunked out of elementary school: no wealthy or influential connections can help you now. Here all that matters is what *you* are, and we learn to recognize character and to respect it, above mere size or strength or intellect, in even the puniest and most seasick among us. . . .

Hundreds of episodes like this, in scores of little ships, shaped the character and outlook of thousands of young Canadians in the Second World War. This is the story of some of those episodes, of some of those men in some of those ships, especially in those parts of the great oceans that wash Canada's shores.

Roll Along

IT WAS in a remote corner of Bedford Basin that Prince Andrew found us: a little Second World War corvette tucked away behind the lines of NATO frigates and guided-missile destroyers he had come to review. With a party of naval veterans aboard, HMCS *Sackville*, the last corvette, miraculously restored to her wartime configuration, had been towed out to lie in line with her modern sisters for a ceremonial inspection to mark the seventy-fifth birthday of what had once been the Royal Canadian Navy.

Smart and gleaming in white paint, the Governor General's reviewing vessel, *Quest*, glided past in a shrilling of bosun's pipes and a snapping of salutes. After a first incredulous glance at our Western Approaches camouflage, young Andrew, himself a naval officer, grinned from ear to ear and gave us an enthusiastic wave. Amongst all the state-of-the-art warships of the NATO fleet he had recognized us, and honoured us, for what we were, a marvellous survival from an older, grimmer age, and the embodiment of Canada's naval heritage.

All that weekend hundreds of us, grizzled veterans of a forgotten war, had wandered the streets of a Halifax magically transformed from the ramshackle wartime port we had known into one of Canada's loveliest cities. Even the dockyard was unrecognizable; Jetty Five was no longer the old corvette berth of the wartime years, and the ships lying there, with their wizard weaponry merely so many bumps and blisters in their topsides save for a popgun on the fo'c'sle, seemed disappointingly bland and innocuous to eyes accustomed to the belligerent silhouettes of the Second World War Tribal destroyers whose names they bore.

Below decks, the comfort and convenience bore no relation to the Spartan messdecks of our day, just as the pallid people — many of them wearing spectacles and moustaches! — peering into their vast displays of console screens and dials seemed a race apart from the tough, sea-hardened crews of our primitive corvettes.

It may have been partly the uniforms, with everyone in square rig of drab green, that set this new navy apart from the one we had known. Or it may have been the proliferation of servicewomen (an aggressively masculine lot they seemed nowadays, nothing like the Jenny Wren of our day, who always managed to retain her feminine charm whatever rig she wore). But mostly it was technological change that made today's seagoing navy so different from ours; radar had brought everyone below decks from the windswept bridges of our era, and allowed ships to be worked and fought in air-conditioned comfort.

It remained for the naval tattoo that evening to put things in perspective, and link our antediluvian navy with this new space-age service. For there was a gun run, and, by all that's holy, with the same old twelve-pounders of our day, of our father's day! All those husky young matelots, in bell-bottoms and flannels, manhandling the heavy gun-carriages with speed and precision, were unchanged from the young sailors we had sailed with, and when the bands paraded in traditional navy blue, gaitered legs moving as one and tape ribbons flying to the wonderful old naval march "Hearts of Oak", we could feel our own heart pound with pride.

Moments later, the bands played themselves out of the arena to the tune of "Roll Along, Wavy Navy, Roll Along", and we were glad of the merciful darkness that hid the moisture in our eyes, for that song, roared out years ago in innumerable bar-rooms, crowded trains, and midnight liberty boats, was *our* song, the theme of the Coca-Cola sailors, the corvette navy that won the war at sea. More than anything else could have done, it recalled the spirit of an age, the spirit of a fleet and a service and a nation that was uniquely Canadian.

It is that spirit, proud and just a touch defiant of the established order of things, that links our old navy with the new. More than uniform, ritual, or tradition, that spirit is the true legacy from Canada's wartime past.

The Triangle Run

THE BATTLEFIELD

TO THE MODERN traveller, journeying by air between North America and Britain or Europe, the North Atlantic is simply a bore, a tedious stretch of several hours, to be made as painless as possible with in-flight movies, a meal or two, and something from the bar. Few, if any, passengers are aware that the featureless grey sea occasionally glimpsed through the thick cloud cover was an enormous battlefield, the site of one of the longest, bloodiest, and most decisive battles in all history. In fact, the jet aircraft of today follows the same great-circle routes between the New World and the Old along which the convoys plodded in the Second World War. This is the field on which the six-year Battle of the Atlantic was fought out; directly below today's jaded planeloads of passengers the ocean floor is paved with the wrecks of the more than six thousand merchant ships sunk in that struggle, and with them, buried in the eternal darkness of the ocean depths, lie the bones of the more than 40,000 merchant seamen who died in them.

There is, of course, nothing to mark their graves, or those of 28,000 young men still entombed in their "iron coffins" — the 785 German U-boats sunk while preying upon them — or of the thousands of sailors in the escort ships lost fighting the convoys through. Merchant sailor and naval seaman, Allied and

Axis, they lie forever in the common anonymity of the ocean deeps, and rare indeed is the passenger today who reflects that his freedom to fly wherever and whenever he wishes may have been won for him by the sacrifice of those young men whose bones lie so far below him.

For Canadian travellers, this watery battlefield has particular significance. It is not simply a matter of the human cost — some two thousand of the youngsters lying in those shattered wrecks are Canadians — but the fact that it was in the Battle of the Atlantic that Canada achieved its finest hour. For the last two years of the Second World War, Canada took over responsibility for all North Atlantic trade convoy operation, and from June 1944 until the end of the war Canadian warships provided the entire close escort for all trans-Atlantic convoys, as well as a large proportion of the support groups. This enormous undertaking, involving a naval force of more than three hundred ships, was an unprecedented achievement for a small nation that had entered the war with a six-ship navy, and it marked both Canada's greatest single contribution to the Allied war effort and the nation's proudest moment as a major member of the free world powers.

There is yet another aspect of the Battle of the Atlantic of which few Canadians are aware. Of all the battles of the Second World War, it was the only one which saw Canadians killed right in Canada, not merely off its ocean coasts but right in the Canadian heartland. For the first time since the Fenian raids of the previous century, enemy forces set foot on Canadian soil. They built sophisticated installations on Canadian territory, and roamed at will up and down Canada's mightiest river, sinking Canadian ships and killing Canadian seamen in full view of helpless Canadian householders on shore. If the Battle of the

Atlantic marked Canada's greatest triumph, it was also the occasion of the nation's most humiliating debacle.

Although this tremendous maritime conflict raged, with varying intensity, from one side of the Atlantic to the other during the course of its six-year length, nowhere was it fought more bitterly or under more trying conditions than in Canadian waters. It was in these waters that Allied shipping was concentrated; it was from Canadian ports that most Allied trans-Atlantic trade convoys sailed; it was the terrible Canadian winter on rockbound Canadian coasts that took the worst toll of Allied ships and men and tested merchant and naval crews alike to the limits of their endurance.

This is the story of Canada's own Atlantic battle, a part of a wider conflict but fought under distinctive regional conditions which imparted a special flavour to every aspect of its operations. Its boundaries were sharply limited: to the north and west by the coastline of Canada and Newfoundland, to the south by New York's Long Island, and to the eastward by an artificial point south of Cape Farewell in Greenland and east of Cape Race in Newfoundland, drawn on a chart and designated as Western Ocean Meeting Point, or, more simply, Westomp. It was here at Westomp that escort ships operating from Canadian mainland ports handed over the screening of eastbound convoys to the mid-ocean escort groups, based at St. John's, Newfoundland, and it was here that they met westbound convoys and relieved their mid-ocean escorts for the voyage on to North American destinations.

Westomp was nothing, a pencil mark on a chart, a mere patch of featureless grey ocean, but it loomed large in the lives of Canadian navy men for endless wartime years. Sometimes it beckoned as a goal to be reached, where responsibilities could be shucked off and the memories of frightful weather or ferocious U-boats could be forgotten in the anticipation of a run ashore and a peaceful night's sleep alongside a quiet, and motionless, wharf. Sometimes it was a rendezvous to be dreaded, where a scattered convoy, broken by the devastating onslaught of a fierce enemy or fiercer weather, had to be rounded up and re-formed to meet the challenge of what lay ahead.

Within this regional battleground, Canadian escort ships operated what was officially known as the Western Local Escort Force, and bureaucrats were fond of addressing signals to the "WLEF", but no seaman in the Halifax groups would dream of such a reference. For him, and for the crews of escort ships everywhere, this was "The Triangle Run", and everyone engaged in it took a perverse pride in the hardships to be endured and the handicaps to be borne by everyone unfortunate enough to be associated with it.

The "Triangle" had evolved from a simpler run; in the early months of the war it was found expedient to break up the long haul from America to Britain into shorter segments, and Canadian escorts simply provided cover for a few hundred miles to convoys sailing from Halifax and Sydney bound eastward, and covered the same sector for convoys arriving from the United Kingdom. The Americans got into the act in the fall of 1941 and, although officially still neutral, took over the screening of all convoys sailing out of Halifax, leaving the British and the Canadians with only the Sydney convoys to worry about. But this peculiar arrangement had gone out the window when the Japanese destroyed the U.S. fleet at Pearl Harbor in December 1941. The Yanks immediately pulled up stakes; within a matter of weeks every U.S. naval vessel had left the Atlantic for the Pacific theatre or their own east-coast areas, leaving only two Coast Guard cutters behind to fly the Stars and Stripes on the convoy routes. The Royal Canadian Navy, growing steadily as the first of what was to be a flood of escort vessels joined the fleet from busy shipyards on the Great Lakes and both coasts, resumed responsibility for escort of the Halifax and Sydney convoys, and watched in horror and amazement the tragedy unfolding to the south.

Admiral E. J. King, commanding the U.S. navy, had made a disastrous decision: in the teeth of all Allied advice and wartime experience, he discarded the convoy system for "offensive patrols", and left the ships of the huge coastal trade and the vital oil run from South America to manage on their own as best they could. It was the worst blunder of the war, and it nearly proved fatal. Before convoys were reinstituted, literally hundreds of ships, including the all-important oil tankers, were sunk every month within ten miles of the U.S. coast. Every German U-boat available was sent to take part in the slaughter—their "Happy Time"; they were present in such numbers off Cape Hatteras that they burned orange running lights while on the surface to avoid colliding with one another. The fatuity and conceit of an American admiral cost thousands of lives, and hundreds of ships, and came close to giving Hitler the victory he desperately sought in his submarine campaign against Atlantic shipping.

When, in the nick of time, King admitted defeat and the convoy system was introduced, bit by bit, along the U.S. coast, the Triangle Run came into being. Canadian escort groups sailed from Halifax eastbound with fast convoys, and from Sydney in Cape Breton with slow convoys, handing over their charges at Westomp to the mid-ocean groups, then heading for St. John's to refuel before picking up a westbound convoy and escorting it to Boston or New York. Following a run ashore they would pick up a convoy there for delivery to Halifax and begin the whole cycle all over again.

You had some things going for you on the Triangle Run. It lacked the glamour of the St. John's–Londonderry operation, the "Newfy–Derry run", and those mid-ocean types were always swanking about in their Gieves-tailored uniforms and spinning salty dips about Irish girls and Guinness, but for a run ashore there was nothing to touch New York. No sailor would ever forget his first view of Manhattan from the sea.

It began a long way out, with the lightship marking the Ambrose shoals and the appearance of the first blimps. Short of long-range reconnaissance aircraft, the U.S. navy had turned to lighter-than-air blimps for aerial patrolling, and these strange apparitions were a peculiar part of the offshore scene at a busy port like New York. These vast gasbags, with a little gondola suspended beneath, seemed almost uncontrollable in any sort of wind, and their jerky movements when descending to investigate something beneath them, plus their apparent vulnerability, made them suspect in the eyes of escort commanders busily shepherding their flocks of recalcitrant merchantmen into single file for the long parade into harbour. (Signal, from destroyer to blimp: "KEEP YOUR DISTANCE; I'VE GOT A PIN.")

And then, while still away out to sea, it would happen. Over the horizon, right ahead, you'd catch a glimpse of something that became clearer with every minute. It couldn't be, surely not, but yes, by God, it was: that amazing, unbelievable skyline, made familiar by all the movies and pictures and postcards; there they were, poking right up above the horizon, the incredible towers of New York City!

As you got closer and could examine the scene with binoculars, you could pick out individual landmarks, buildings that up to then had been only so many names. There, surely, was the Empire State tower, and the Chrysler Building; that must be Radio City, and over there . . . It was thrilling to see the actual buildings behind these familiar names, and as one entered the harbour itself and confronted the stunning reality of Manhattan Island close-to on the starboard side, with the Statue of Liberty lifting her gigantic torch just over there, it was like wandering onto a stage set for some great and familiar play. There it was, just as advertised, but it took a little while to accept it all as real.

We found our way to the escort berths on Staten Island, across the harbour from the city itself, in a sort of daze. It was only after cleaning up the ship and taking on fuel and supplies, and then piling ashore with overnight leave, that we began to realize just how far we were from the centre of things. You climbed aboard the *Gold Star Mother*, as the ferryboat was named, a legacy from Mayor LaGuardia's campaign to encourage motherhood, and settled in for a long but fascinating trip through a harbour crammed with exotic shipping, much of it enormous and bearing famous names, for all the big liners were regular callers and there was always a hulking British or American battleship or two under repair at the Navy Yard.

But the long, long subway ride after that wasn't much fun; the shabby cars, the noise, the zombie-like night people on the return run — none of this was the stuff of dreams. However, the city itself more than made up for the hours of tedious travel; for a fellow from Brandon or Oshawa, accustomed to the tacky delights of Slackers or Newfyjohn, the realities of Manhattan night-life were almost too much. Big-league sport at Yankee Stadium or the Garden; hundreds of pretty girls, and maybe even a Hollywood starlet or two, to dance with at the enormous USO; all the big bands with the big names at the famous clubs;

Satchmo or Eddie Condon, the Famous Door or the Copacabana or the Latin Quarter — the choices were overwhelming.

Not the least of the wonderful surprises the city had in store was how little everything seemed to cost a serviceman. After Halifax, where men in uniform were second-class citizens to be overcharged in grubby restaurants and pushed back into queues outside overcrowded theatres, New York hospitality was a revelation. In bars you would be welcomed as a "hee-ro" and treated to free drinks; in restaurants and night-clubs you were given priority over mere civilians.

Nobody savoured the pleasures of the city more than Hal Lawrence, then a young sub-lieutenant RCNVR. As Lawrence recalled it:

> Harry James was playing his golden trumpet at the Taft Hotel; at the Starlight Room of the Waldorf-Astoria we would dance to Xavier Cugat; at other hotels to Jimmy Dorsey, Tommy Dorsey, Glenn Miller, and Benny Goodman — "Chattanooga Choo-Choo", "String of Pearls", "The Jersey Bounce", "Brazil", "Tuxedo Junction".
>
> Do some of you remember the girls of 1939? Saddle shoes, bobby sox, flaring skirts just below the knee, "sloppy-joe" sweaters with sleeves pushed up below the elbow, long, loose hair, flashing brown legs, and flushed faces, and bright eyes. They danced to the soaring virtuosity of Goodman's clarinet, the confident authority of James' trumpet, the mellow trombone of Dorsey in "I'm Getting Sentimental Over You", or the sweet nostalgia of Miller's "Moonlight Serenade". And the couples would melt together so you couldn't tell where he ended and she began, and the lights would dim, and the hall would be silent

> except for the aching beauty of fifty musicians playing their hearts out. Life was unbearably sweet and you dimly perceived it would not always be thus.

Ah, it was heady stuff, and it was just as well that New York turn-arounds were notoriously brief and efficient. Only the duty watch got much sleep in New York, but it left a fellow with warm memories to cherish, peering over the dodger into a stinging snowstorm as his ship chivvied yet another gaggle of ungainly merchantmen into some sort of shape for the outward-bound convoy.

Boston, the other assembling-point for ships bound north and east, was a pale shadow of its larger neighbour as a liberty port, but it gave a sense of history, with all its Revolutionary landmarks, and there were always the Red Sox at Fenway Park or the Bruins in the funny old arena and vintage burlesque at the Old Howard. On a scale of one to ten, Boston rated about seven.

By way of contrast, St. John's in Newfoundland, or Newfyjohn as it was universally known, was a difficult port of call to evaluate. On the one hand, its physical attractions were strictly limited; once you had visited the Sterling Café, a couple of barnlike theatres, and the Movie Chat tearoom, you had just about exhausted the flesh-pots of the place, which were hardly on a par with those of Sodom or Gomorrah. But on the other hand it was the next best thing to home; the Newfies really put themselves out to make visiting sailors feel one of the family, and the place fairly jumped with organized activity. There were nightly dances with lots of local girls to dance with and refreshments laid on by the hard-working matrons of the town, and the Caribou Club, the K of C hall, and the Salvation Army gave lonely matelots a variety of places to go on a run ashore. And for officers there was The Crowsnest, the famous Seagoing Officers Club, an old loft reached by a spindly staircase of fifty-nine steps, with walls literally covered with the unofficial crests of the destroyers and corvettes of the Newfoundland Escort Force. An ideal place to drop in for a scrambled-egg sandwich before a movie, or for a convivial evening with fellows from other ships in port, and if half the stories told around the bar of U-boat sinkings had been true, Hitler would have thrown in the towel long before.

But it was the hospitality of its individual citizens that made the ramshackle old town, its wooden houses crammed along steep streets on the hillside leading up from the harbour, such a memorable place for prairie youngsters far from home. Just about everyone you met would invite you in for dinner or a "cuppa", and this was no perfunctory gesture. A high-school teacher who invited me into his home for a family meal, right off the street, wrote regularly until his death thirty years later. With its stark surroundings and terrible weather, Newfyjohn was no bed of roses, but everyone on the Triangle Run cherished warm memories of the place.

But it was as a naval base that St. John's made its greatest contribution to the war at sea. Admiral L. W. Murray as Flag Officer, Newfoundland, and Captain Rollo Mainguy as his Captain (D) formed a team that did much to impart a unique atmosphere to the base. There was not a great deal to it physically; the navy took over the top floor of the Newfoundland Hotel, on its hillside overlooking the harbour, for its administrative offices, and a Royal Navy submarine depot ship, originally HMS *Forth* and later the ancient HMS *Greenwich*, was berthed on the south side of the harbour to provide workshop facilities, and that was about it. However, Mainguy and Murray brought in a staff of exceptionally gifted and dedicated officers and men, inspired them with the notion that the base was there to serve the needs of the ships, and not the other way around as was common to other naval bases, and made it the most efficient of all the Atlantic escort ports.

And the harbour itself was like no other place on earth. From seaward, you approached what appeared to be an unbroken iron-bound shore, the narrow entrance only revealing itself from very close in. You passed through a narrow gut beneath beetling cliffs, with a distinctive stone structure, the Cabot Tower, atop the hill on the right. Once you were through the narrow entrance, the harbour opened up, a sort of water-filled crater within a mountain, with rows of wooden houses, painted every shade of the rainbow, straggling up the steep hillside on the right hand, topped by the twin timber towers of the old cathedral.

Fronting the city waterfront was a row of ancient finger piers, with even older ships — sealers, Banks schooners, coastal steamers — lying alongside. Right ahead, at the top of the harbour, was a shipyard of sorts with a handful of merchantmen under the cranes in varying states of disrepair, and all along the left-hand side was a string of barn-like warehouses and fish plants, with a nest of oil-storage tanks crowning the hillside above. It was here, on the celebrated South Side, that the escort berths were, and the salt-stained hulls of ancient destroyers, of jaunty fat-funnelled corvettes and slab-sided minesweepers, were nested up, three and four deep, along the rickety piers owned by Bowring and Cashin and Harvey and other well-known Newfy trading families.

Clutter the centre of the harbour with storm-battered merchant ships, many of them war-damaged and awaiting repair, fill the air with the clamour of seagulls and the hoots of harbour-craft and perfume it with the all-pervasive stink of fish and fuel oil, and you have Newfyjohn, home from home, and any sailor off the Newfy–Derry or Triangle runs could conjure it up in any part of the world by simply closing his eyes.

But Halifax, of course, was what the Triangle Run was all about. More than just a port of call, it was home for all the escort groups operating the West Atlantic convoys, and the base for a large fleet of ships of every imaginable sort, ranging from former luxury yachts to elderly destroyers and coal-burning minesweepers. Halifax was "Slackers", the universal and disparaging name for HMCS *Stadacona*, the naval shore establishment; it was the "East Coast port" the newspapers were always referring to, the assembly point for all but the slowest of eastbound trade convoys and the port of embarkation for thousands of Canadian servicemen proceeding overseas. It was Canada's principal operational base, with active artillery defences, busy air-force fields, and enormous hutments of every sort to provide temporary accommodation for large bodies of men.

Buried under a wartime accretion of makeshift buildings and emergency construction were the skeletal remains of a charming, historic capital city, still visible in the lovely tree-shaded boulevards, lined with old and enormous frame homes, the public gardens, the shoreside parks, and the Georgian jewel-box that is Province House. Unfortunately the infrastructure of this little provincial capital was totally inadequate to cope with the floods of uniformed servicemen that engulfed it. Thousands of young men from all over Canada were shipped there, for service or training or embarkation, and were turned loose nightly to seek what relaxation they could find in the mean and shabby streets of downtown Halifax. A pleasant restaurant, the Green Lantern, and an attractive theatre, the Capitol, laid out inside like a medieval castle complete with drawbridge, were quickly overrun, along with the lovely lounges of the Lord Nelson and the lively ballroom of the Nova Scotian, the city's two hotels of any size. Most homesick servicemen were forced to find what solace they could in the jam-packed wet canteens in barracks or in the various dens and dives of the squalid slums. Not surprisingly, the city was disliked by most of the thousands of servicemen who passed through it and saw only the ramshackle streetcars, the crowded cafés, and the down-at-heel old wooden houses lining the pot-holed streets of the meaner sections of the city.

For men living aboard ships based there, Halifax had an added quality. The naval base, unlike the wartime installations elsewhere, was a permanent, peacetime establishment, and tended to regard the flood of emergency warships and "Hostilities Only" personnel that had engulfed it as a sort of temporary aberration, an affliction to be borne until happier times returned and ratings once again were fellows who knew their place, and naval officers could be expected to marry money and play their proper role in local society. In the meantime, all those damned tinpot little ships cluttering up the wharves and trot-buoys were an infernal nuisance, and the bumptious, ill-trained kids in them were even worse. Official Halifax immediately set about protecting itself, and Halifax port orders and dockyard regulations quickly set limits on where and when men from ships were permitted to go. Offices would only be open between the hours of thus and so, and anyone wishing to see officialdom at any level should apply in writing or perhaps be on the premises, suitably dressed, at a certain hour, when, perhaps, his petty needs might be looked into. Like the Ten Commandments, port orders were strong on "Thou shalt not".

But if the dockyard wore an uninviting aspect for the escorts clustered five and six deep around Jetties Four and Five, the big naval barracks ashore was an even more dismal place. Men under punishment, men in transit, men under training, men awaiting courts or courses mingled with a permanent floating population of men who seemed to be going nowhere at all in this enormous, ill-run establishment. The nickname "Slackers" said it all.

In wartime Halifax there was little of the sense of urgency, of emergency "make-do", of Newfoundland or even of New York or Boston, and certainly there was none of the civilian hospitality, the organized dances and the USOs, of those wartime bases. It was not surprising under the circumstances that Halifax should be disliked by nearly all naval servicemen, officers and men alike, and positively hated by some. This animosity was the single factor that lightened the gloom of a convoy sailing day at the escort berths. It may be blowing and snowing, but at least we're getting out of this dump, right?

Halifax, St. John's, New York, Boston — these were the ports of the Triangle Run. Within the boundaries of its battlefield lay thousands of miles of featureless ocean, dark green in the occasional summer sunshine, a white-flecked grey under the usual North Atlantic overcast, and across this watery waste lay the routes of the great convoys which carried the men and materials of the New World that sustained the Old in its battle against the ferocious forces of Nazi Germany. It was here, in these waters off the east shores of Canada, that thousands of young Canadians endured the most testing ordeal of their lives, an ordeal that might culminate in the sudden terror of a night attack, and agonizing death by drowning in a freezing sea, or might be drawn out over endless days, weeks, months, years of plodding back and forth in atrocious weather without so much as a sight or sound of an elusive enemy. Not the least of the curses of life at sea in convoy escort was the brain-numbing boredom of ploughing interminably across miles of unchanging ocean through an unchanging world, living a life of unvarying routine.

It was a boredom that frequently found expression in signals from one ship to another, and in many groups such signals might be made by sending a biblical reference which, on being looked up, gave suitable expression to the sentiments of the sender. In such groups a Bible and a concordance were essential equipment and were kept handy in the chart-house bookcase, along with the Lights List and the tide-tables. This boredom was never more eloquently expressed or a biblical expression more aptly chosen than in the famous signal from a Canadian escort to its group senior officer after some days of featureless patrolling:

To: HMCS *Coaticook.*

From: HMCS *Levis.*

"13 HEBREWS 8." ("Jesus Christ, the same yesterday, and today, and for ever.")

SHIPS AND MEN

THE PECULIAR circumstances of the Triangle Run — short runs, fast turnarounds — ensured that the escort groups engaged on it would have a distinctive character, setting them apart from the groups engaged on the mid-ocean run, and certainly no ships contributed more to the unique flavour of life on the Triangle than what were officially known as the Town-class destroyers. With their distinctive four thin funnels set atop a long, narrow-gutted, flush-decked hull, "like a packet of fags on a pencil", these marvellous monsters were universally known as "four-stackers", and no other naval vessel ever launched was more heartily cursed or more perversely beloved.

Built as part of a First World War program for the U.S. navy, they had been laid up for decades before being handed over to the British in the fall of 1940 in the celebrated "destroyers for bases" deal, the most dubious gift since the Greeks left that wooden horse to the Trojans. Inherently unstable, designed to slice through seas rather than over them, they were appalling sea-boats in North Atlantic weather, and their ancient machinery, fragile at the best of times, was simply incapable of standing up to the demands made upon it by wartime conditions. Leaving six for Canada, the hard-pressed British originally took forty-four to replace their destroyer losses sustained in the Norway campaign and in Mediterranean convoys, but, quickly appreciating the poor hand they'd been dealt, they discarded two — *Buxton* and *Hamilton* — to the Canadians, *Lincoln* to the Norwegians, and *Garland* and *Burza* to the Poles, and left a number of others on the American side of the ocean in the hope they might not come to as much harm as on what was then the busier side.

Everything possible was done to improve the stability of these unseaworthy craft. Heavy railway tracks were welded along decks and in bilges, the midship gun mountings and one set of torpedo tubes were removed from the upper deck, and some of the plating was cut from the towering topsides, but as fast as topweight was removed, more was added by the accumulation of new developments — radar aerials, ahead-throwing weapons, bridge-houses. In a head sea their forward gun was unworkable on its wave-swept fo'c'sle, while a quartering sea would cause such a rolling pitch that both screws would be exposed. They were, in short, absolute bitches, yet perversely their crews often adored them, for they had good central heating and boasted bunks instead of the more practical hammocks of other RN and RCN ships.

But what made the four-stackers proverbial on the Triangle Run was their propensity for getting into difficulties, usually of the most expensive kind. *Annapolis* quickly burned out a boiler and was reduced to three funnels, an omission as noticeable as a missing front tooth. *Columbia* made herself unique by crashing into a cliff without touching bottom; *Cauldwell* once immobilized herself by ramming a whale; *Buxton* was scarcely ever out of dockyard hands; *Hamilton* (named for the Bermuda town) collided with her sister, HMS *Georgetown*, immediately on arrival for operations at St. John's and, undocking after lengthy repairs, ran aground and had to go back in dock. Turned loose at last, she accidentally sank a Dutch (friendly) submarine and was banished to Digby, Nova Scotia, as a training ship in 1943 before she could do further harm. *St. Clair* put herself out of business by ramming the tanker *Clam* on arrival in St. John's and ended her days as a harbour hulk training the navy's fire-fighters. Even her earlier moment of triumph had had an odd flavour to it: she had had to sink the abandoned hulk of the British destroyer *Mashona* by torpedo after the two had been subjected to an intensive air attack, and then pick up her survivors.

Most of the glory won by the four-stackers was achieved by the "long-leggers", the handful that had been fitted with extra fuel tankage and were thus able to operate on the mid-ocean run. *St. Croix*, the most famous of them all, sank *U-90* and *U-87* before herself falling victim to an acoustic torpedo. Other notable losses included brave *Broadway*, sunk by a torpedo attack in wild weather, and another RN ship, HMS *Belmont*, blown up with the loss of all hands a few hours out of Halifax harbour.

One way or another, four-stackers seemed to be the centre of most of the yarns spun in wet canteens or around The Crowsnest bar, and they became an integral part of Triangle Run folklore. They had a good turn of speed and boasted some torpedo "clout", but, above all, they were the only destroyers available. In the long run they earned their keep, and, with the more sophisticated River-class destroyers busy elsewhere, the four-stackers took over as senior officers' ships for just about all local escort groups; their distinctive silhouette, with their four pipes sticking up over the horizon, became a familiar part of the scenery as they zigzagged across the front of every convoy on the Triangle Run.

Yet an even more distinctive ship in all Triangle escort groups was the Bangor. Designed as fast fleet minesweepers for the

Royal Navy, Bangors were originally introduced into the Canadian navy to cope with the large number of mines expected to be sown by U-boats in Canada's vulnerable estuaries and harbour approaches. However, only a handful of such mines were ever laid, and the regular sweep of the Halifax approaches became the chore of the little coal-burning Comox-class minesweepers, later supplemented by a handful of wooden-hulled vessels sweeping for magnetic and acoustic mines. This latter type of sweep was called the "double l" or "LL" sweep, and in a fit of bravado the RCN determined to give ships fitted for such sweeping names that began with two l's. But, after christening the *Llewellyn* and the *Lloyd George*, the naval names committee lost its nerve and opted to name the rest after Canadian villages. There were many in the service who considered the committee had chickened out far too hastily, and who whiled away many a bar-room hour by devising suitable names for the rest of the ten-ship class. (Let's see now: there's Lloydminster and Llangollen and . . .)

Freed of any need to sweep mines, the numerous Bangors being turned out by Canadian shipyards east and west were fitted out as escort vessels, the type of ship most desperately needed, and, although never intended for the job, they did it surprisingly well.

They were steel single-funnelled steamships just over one hundred and eighty feet long, and their twin screws and shallow draught made them even more manoeuvrable than a corvette. Their machinery was a good deal more sophisticated than the simple corvette installations, with Admiralty three-drum boilers operating under forced draught and their twin engines giving them the same sixteen-knot performance as their larger contemporary. But their bluff bows, short fo'c'sle, and lack of flare and sheer made them uncomfortable in a seaway, and they lacked the fuel capacity necessary for the long mid-ocean runs. Though chunky and flat-sided, for they had to accommodate everyone above the waterline when sweeping, they had a purposeful look about them and could enchant even a grizzled old salt of twenty-three like me, with nearly three years' sea time behind him.

I first saw HMCS *Minas*, a steam Bangor (there were also shorter diesel-driven editions), refitting in Dalhousie, New Brunswick. She lay alongside the paper-company wharf on a sunny summer afternoon, grubby with the grime of refit, her decks festooned with innumerable power cables and cluttered with fitments being added on and others being removed, her sides blotchy with red lead where working parties had been removing patches of rust. In dowdy dishabille, like an old maid in nightgown and curlers, she lay with all her defects laid bare, and I loved every inch of her, for she was mine, all mine. She was my first command, and I stood in the weeds on the other side of the little basin and drank in every detail.

She had been built as a unit of the permanent navy and had been finished with an attention to detail and quality that set her apart from the wartime emergency corvettes I was accustomed to, and I positively gloated over the little touches here and there that reflected "class". There was her Thornycroft funnel, cowled and flat-sided, like those of the big destroyers and cruisers; her name, in raised letters of heavy bronze, on each quarter; the solid brass footplates engraved with her name at each gangway; the long, uncluttered quarterdeck and the airy wardroom opening onto it, vastly different from the stuffy lower-deck hutch we were accustomed to in corvettes. Oh, she was beautiful, right enough, and after I'd gone aboard and revelled in the captain's quarters under the bridge — a spacious blue-carpeted cabin with a settee, a desk, a washbasin, and no fewer than *five* curtained ports opening on the upper deck, and a snug little chart-room, complete with sea-berth, next door — I wouldn't have traded my new command for a battleship. True, you had to walk the length of the ship to the wardroom head whenever nature called (they'd taken over the captain's bathroom to house the new radar set), and you had to hang out one of the salt-stained windows of the enclosed bridge, designed for minesweeping rather than escort, to get a proper look around, but you can't have everything.

When *Minas* finally put to sea to rejoin her mates on the Triangle Run, gleaming in fresh paint, with her teak gundeck and quarterdeck freshly scrubbed and a clean white ensign flying from her tripod mainmast, she exuded all the pride and panache of a brand-new cruiser. Bring on your war!

Yet despite the four-stack destroyers and the Bangor escorts, the real strength of the Triangle Run escort force, like that of the mid-ocean groups, lay in the ubiquitous corvette. From first to last, the bulk and backbone of every convoy escort was this remarkable vessel, as unique a product of the Second World War as the Liberty Ship or the Flying Fortress.

A British design, intended originally as a stopgap coastal escort, the corvette was pressed by wartime shortages into ocean escort work, where her amazing good qualities suddenly became manifest. Just over two hundred feet long, with compound triple-expansion engines driving her single screw, she was easy, quick, and cheap to build, even in places where no ship had ever been built before, and she was turned out by the hundreds in Britain and Canada, becoming the largest class of warship ever launched.

Designed along the lines of a northern trawler, she showed her origins in her flared bows, bold sheer, and duck stern, and was an outstanding, if lively, sea-boat, capable of weathering any Atlantic gale. Originally intended to carry half a hundred men, she eventually accommodated twice that number, who were needed to man her ever-growing armament and instrumentation. Her main armament was the depth-charge, which she fired in diamond-shaped patterns of up to ten at a time from twin traps in the stern and twin mortars on each quarter. She also carried a four-inch gun forward, a pair of rapid-firing Oerlikon cannon in the bridge wings, a two-pounder pom-pom, and a searchlight in an after "bandstand" set above the quarterdeck. With good radar and asdic, or sonar as it was later called, she was a remarkably useful little warship, with a surprising fuel capacity giving her ample range and a top speed of sixteen knots, frequently exceeded in service. But her most valuable quality was her turning circle, tightest of all Allied warships, and, most importantly, tighter than that of a submerged U-boat. In any submarine confrontation, the corvette was the manoeuvring master.

In a real sense, the corvette was *the* North Atlantic close escort ship from late 1941 to the end of the war. However, in the spring of 1942, the testing time for escorts on the Triangle Run, the corvettes, Bangors, and four-stackers were operating at far from peak efficiency, mainly because of inadequate equipment.

Throughout the war, Canadian ships lagged behind their British and, later, U.S. contemporaries in fittings, equipment, and weapons. By mid-war, all Royal Navy corvettes had extended forecastles, which greatly increased both habitability and sea-keeping, and most had bridge Oerlikons, bandstand pom-poms, 271 radar, sophisticated asdic, and sometimes "Huff-Duff" or high-frequency direction-finding sets, as well as the hedgehog, an ahead-throwing weapon that allowed asdic contact to be maintained throughout an attack. Canadian ships had none of these, apart from what could be scrounged by individual ships during visits to U.K. ports. Some Canadian ships carried their short fo'c'sles and primitive weaponry right through to the war's end. From first to last, Canadians were the backward boys of the escort groups, making do with primitive instrumentation and obsolete weaponry while envying the state-of-the-art devices sported by their British and American cousins.

Canada, with a population of only fourteen million, was fully stretched to cope with the needs of an expanding navy, let alone the army and the air force, and this difficulty in maintaining its forces was aggravated by a narrow nationalism in Ottawa that prevented the hard-pressed services from taking advantage of weapons available to them from their allies. There were Canadian corvettes, for example, mounting a pair of twin Lewis machine-guns on the bandstand intended for a pom-pom, and Browning machine-guns in the bridge wings instead of the Oerlikon cannon of their British contemporaries, although both pom-poms and Oerlikons were available in the British dockyards where they berthed. "Buy Canadian" was the rule, and Canadian sailors ruefully made do with thin Canadian paint, for instance, that flaked in bad weather or turned black in cold, instead of the heavy and durable paints available in British and American yards.

But the most punishing penalty of this nationalistic policy was in the field of radar, where it was to cost the loss of ships and men, and allow many a U-boat to escape unscathed.

Radar was a pre-war development; Watson-Watt had produced his invention in time to have it incorporated in a chain of land-based radar stations that helped RAF pilots win the Battle of Britain. Small ship-borne sets became possible when John Randal and Harry Boot invented the magnetron in November 1939, and the Royal Navy was running secret tests in 1940 that showed that the 271, as the ship set was called, could detect the periscope tip of a submerged submarine at a distance of half a mile, and a trimmed-down submarine at far greater ranges, depending on the state of the sea. But the biggest advantage of the 271 set was that it greatly shortened the operating wavelength, and consequently the length of the aerial required, allowing it to become so small that it could be "brought inside" and housed in a Perspex bubble that, placed on top of the operator's cabin, became the distinctive "lighthouse" of the 271 radar set. This was the set that won the war at sea, and by 1942 it was in common use in British escort groups.

Initially it was viewed with suspicion by seamen in ships where it was first installed. Noting that ratings were reluctant to go aloft, especially to the crow's-nest just above the radar dome, the captain of a ship in which a new 271 radar had just been installed questioned a dilatory seaman as to the reason. After a certain amount of bashful toe-stubbing, the sailor confessed that the buzz was that rays from the set would make a man impotent. Nipping an incipient problem in the bud, the quick-witted captain declared the rumour to be nonsense; radar rays, he maintained, made a man temporarily sterile, not impotent. Viewed thus, it could be seen by any seagoing Lothario that the thing was rather more of a bonus than a drawback; performance was not affected and there would be no bothersome after-effects to worry about. The 271 radar became the most popular piece of equipment in the ship.

But Canadian groups, by comparison, were cursed with the SW1C, a peculiar Canadian development that featured a rotating rake-type "yagi" aerial at the masthead, driven by a set of pipes that extended the full length of the mast and was everywhere known as "the plumber's nightmare". This Rube Goldberg affair was led through a series of sharp bends and turns into the operator's cabin, where it was rotated by a Chevrolet steering wheel.

The difficulties posed by the plumber's nightmare were obvious enough; the stresses and strains of rotating a mast-top aerial from such a distance were extreme, and when the pitching and rolling movements of the ship, and the effects of high winds and, above all, of severe winter icing, were added, the whole thing became manifestly impracticable — yet still Ottawa authority persisted. To compound the curse of the wretched aerial drive, the coaxial cable that it housed had to be "purged" periodically, and while the gas bottle that did this was accommodated in the operator's cabin, the pet-cock that had to be turned to vent it was located — where else? — at the top of the mast. Clambering aloft in a midnight blizzard to vent the aerial was an experience that must still haunt the nightmares of former Canadian naval radar operators.

Yet our radar types were nothing if not keen; one of them, an old schoolmate, wearing the distinctive green cloth of his dreadful calling between his lieutenant's stripes, stood on the wheel-house roof throughout a midnight Cape Cod blizzard rotating our broken aerial by hand with a Stillson wrench as we groped our way through an oncoming convoy, being rewarded and revived by five successive hot buttered rums in the wardroom upon arrival. Ah, there were giants in those days!

But difficult though the aerial was — its rake-like "yagi" was supposed to have been named for a Japanese physicist, and everyone knew whose side *he* was on — the real curse of the SW1C was its poor bearing sensitivity and its propensity to give "back echoes", which meant that any blip detected on its glowing green screen might lie in almost any direction or perhaps not exist at all. The effects of this lack of clear information on the peace of mind of a harassed captain conning his ship through a difficult passage can be imagined, and to top everything, the huge ground pulse of the set meant that it could detect nothing within half a mile of the ship, the most vital zone of all for an escort in close contact with a convoy.

Quite apart from the innumerable U-boat contacts which escaped unnoticed in the "grass" or sea clutter of tiny green bumps on the SW1C's glowing screen, the set was the active cause of many serious accidents and collisions, putting some ships high and dry aground and ramming others into cliffs and other unyielding objects. What was most infuriating, however, for the officer of the watch was to spend hours alertly peering into the dark vainly searching for targets reported by the SW1C, only to have something large and substantial — a ship, say, or a large iceberg — go streaming by unannounced at close quarters and then find the operator was unable to detect it on his wretched set. Ice was a particular problem for the SW1C; it would strain at a gnat and swallow a whale. On a clear, sunny day off the Labrador coast for example, it might detect a tiny piece of floating slush at an amazingly long range, and then at midnight fail to detect an approaching berg the size of the Empire State Building.

The SW1C was a curse and an abomination, and until the RCN eventually swallowed its pride and adopted the British 271 set, radar reports were taken with more than a grain of salt by escorts on the Triangle Run.

But the narrow nationalism that inflicted inferior Canadian radar on the Royal Canadian Navy for far too long was only the negative side of a deep national feeling, a compound of a quiet patriotism and a firm belief in the rightness of the Allied cause, a crusade against dictatorship in general and the horrors of Hitler's Nazis in particular. It was this national fervour which kept the navy supplied, from first to last, with a never-failing flow of volunteers, the cream of Canada's young men and, after January 1942, of Canada's young women, too. In that year the Women's Royal Canadian Naval Service was formed, taking over many administrative posts ashore to free men for sea service, and giving hardened naval quartermasters the problems of supplying such exotica as "Bloomers, black, closed at knee". The problems of maintaining a corps of young women in a service hitherto exclusively male naturally enough led to some rather puzzling signals, of which this message to a senior flag officer from the naval training establishment at HMCS *Cornwallis* is typical: "RENEWAL OF STOCKINGS REQUIRED WHITE WOMANS AND SHOES BLACK WOMANS." Just what the Flag Officer, Atlantic, made of this is not known.

The men who manned the escort ships of the Triangle Run were young; almost all were in their late teens or early twenties, and there were even a few sixteen-year-olds passing for eighteen. The insatiable thirst of these Canadian sailors for milk, either "straight" or in milk shakes, appalled their British counterparts and led one commanding officer, a hard-bitten China-coaster, to exclaim: "Haven't any of you Canadians been weaned yet?"

Most lower-deck ratings and almost all the officers were reservists, members of the Royal Canadian Naval Volunteer Reserve, drawn from civilian life, with a leavening of officers of the Royal Canadian Naval Reserve, made up of men from the Merchant Service. A sprinkling of regular-service RCN petty officers and leading hands provided a stiffening in key positions. Senior officers of escorts were often from the permanent force, frequently from Britain's Royal Navy. Indeed, the debt owed to the Royal Navy by the entire Canadian naval establishment was incalculable, for it was the British who provided much of the organization, the training, the equipping, and senior command officers for the fledgling Canadian navy, which at the outbreak of war had comprised six destroyers and a handful of officers and men. It was a debt fully appreciated by men serving at sea, but one not always comprehended by government authority in Ottawa.

From first to last, Canada's naval war effort suffered from the remoteness of the navy's decision-making in Ottawa from its operations at sea. The naval staff, isolated by time and distance in the comfortable confines of Ottawa officialdom, became an extension of wartime federal bureaucracy, far from the harsh realities of the Atlantic war. Canadians serving at sea looked for direction increasingly to British and, later in the war, even to United States authority, which displayed both an obvious grasp of the Atlantic situation and the ability to deal with it, rather than to an NSHQ (Naval Service Headquarters) that was manifestly remote and ineffectual. In a country so physically vast, Ottawa was simply too far from the sea to be the base for a naval headquarters, and this remoteness was a primary cause of the bad decisions and poor staffwork which bedevilled the Royal Canadian Navy.

Ottawa was obsessed with new construction — industrial expansion, jobs, profits, votes — and operations were of secondary concern. Shipyards that could have, should have, been refitting the RCN's hard-driven escort fleet were churning out still more ships, while existing vessels went for years without repairs and modernization. Ships' companies had no sooner shaken down into some sort of competence than their best men would be drafted away to man new construction, to be replaced by still more untrained recruits fresh from the manning pool. While

British and American escorts were formed into stable groups and trained to operate as a unit, Canadian ships operated in ever-changing gaggles, their crews receiving unit training only when in American or British ports with the sophisticated facilities their own bases lacked.

Naval Service Headquarters prided itself on the fantastic expansion of the wartime RCN, and certainly the numbers were impressive. But quantity was at the expense of quality: the ships that were spewed out in such a flood were sent to sea under-armed and ill-equipped, manned by thousands of officers and men woefully short of proper training. Nobody, then or now, seems to have realized the ambitiousness of the Canadian undertaking; the RCN's rate of expansion was fifty to one, compared with the British eight-to-one expansion of its RN, or the Americans' twenty-to-one development of its wartime navy. Australia, in a similar situation to Canada, settled for a four-to-one expansion of its navy. With only one regular-service man in every fifty officers and ratings, the Canadian wartime navy was stretching itself far beyond any reasonable limits, and the price for this Ottawa hubris was paid in much pointless hardship in the North Atlantic.

Canadian sailors, like their counterparts in the other services, were drawn from all walks of life and from all regions of the country, although there tended to be a disproportionate number of volunteers from the Prairie provinces. Indeed, it is probably fair to say that Prairie sailors included many of the best men serving at sea, perhaps because only the most adventurous and enthusiastic of men so far from the sea would volunteer for the navy, and perhaps also because life on the prairie, close to nature, was a better preparation for the harsh realities of life at sea than a more artificial city background.

Although dressed in the traditional uniform common to both the Royal Navy and all other Commonwealth naval services, Canadian sailors had a distinctive identity all their own. For one thing, they tended to be taller than their British counterparts; something to do with better nutrition, perhaps. Drawn from a more mobile society, they were not set apart from their officers by the class distinction so marked in the Royal Navy, and they were unquestionably better educated, the product of a school system with a standard of teaching and rigorous examination beyond anything known in present-day Canada.

But on the negative side Canadian sailors suffered from a crippling defect that seriously hampered their performance in a fighting service. Unused to the restrictions and restraints of life in the highly organized societies and huge cities of older cultures, Canadian youths brought up in the free-and-easy atmosphere of the wide-open spaces and small Canadian towns did not take easily to the confining nature of service life, with its inflexible routine, its insistence on detail, its subservience to authority.

From the beginning, discipline was a major problem in the navy, a problem aggravated by small-ship life and compounded, in the early days when ships were in desperately short supply, by the lack of time to train. Incompetent officers were another contributing factor, many of the newly commissioned officers lacking the moral courage to make unpopular decisions, and former merchant officers failing to appreciate the different standards required by a fighting service. Those standards were assiduously upheld by a corps of hard-bitten gunners' mates in the Halifax gunnery school, presided over by "Old Guts and Gaiters", Gunnery Lieutenant Hugh "Von" Pullen, RCN, who deplored the passing of the cat-o'-nine-tails and flogging as a naval punishment, and declared his firm intention of eating any Germans that came his way. (None, alas, did.)

In the early days of the escort force, it all came down to the commanding officer of individual ships. If he was capable, strict, and fair, his officers and men quickly settled into an efficient and happy unit; if he was not, his ship was scruffy and inefficient, his ship's company quarrelsome and unhappy. There were a good number of such incompetents in such ships. We ran across one once, his ship immobilized in a foreign port, his men idling about the waterfront in every sort of rig, and he himself passing his days and nights in a series of revels and routs financed by the ship's special-contingency fund. He was court-martialled out of the navy and soon became, under a pseudonym, a cultural mandarin at the CBC, his name a byword for the highest artistic and intellectual standards, his cultured accent a model of restrained elegance.

But in a surprisingly short time the realities of life at sea manifested themselves; ships' companies either shaped up or they were unable to ship out. Better training facilities ashore and arduous experience at sea soon produced improved standards of discipline and leadership, and, with their crews shaken down, Canadian ships began to come into their own. The individual ability and initiative of the Canadian sailor were particularly suited to the close team relationships between officers and men engendered by the anti-submarine war, and on the Triangle Run, as in mid-ocean, some Canadian ships soon ranked with the best.

Perhaps the biggest single improvement in the operational efficiency of ocean escorts, ranking with the fitting of the 271 radar sets, was the eventual organization into distinct groups of ships that had formerly operated more or less individually, each group led by a senior officer in a destroyer. This allowed ships to train and operate as a team, and their senior officer could quickly assess the strengths and weaknesses of his group and of individual ships, and take the necessary steps to make his group function as efficiently as possible. Once sufficient escorts were available, this group system was put into effect on the western side of the Atlantic, as it had been already on the British side, and the improvement in every aspect of escort work was immediate and dramatic. Groups were now trained as units at sea and ashore, and convoy screening became a sophisticated business, carried out by men who knew what was expected of them in every contingency.

Not the least of the improvements was in morale. Officers and men quickly responded to the "team feeling", and were eager to display the group marking on their funnels: coloured bands, checkerboard stripes, or the celebrated barber-pole striping of Escort Group C-3. Most groups tended to be known by the nickname of their senior officer's destroyer. In the corvette *Trail* we sailed with the veteran destroyer *Restigouche*, commanded by "Debbie" Piers, and were thus part of "Guts's Group", *Restigouche* being popularly known as "Rustyguts" and, ultimately, merely as "Guts".

Group songs became fashionable when EG 2, the most renowned group of all (led by the fabled Captain Johnny Walker, the world's greatest U-boat killer), adopted the practice of playing "A-hunting We Will Go" over its upper-deck loudspeakers when entering and leaving harbour. This added enormously to group panache and was emulated in other groups, most notably in C-3, where a song celebrating the barber-pole funnel marking, and sung to the tune of "Road to the Isles", was written by Surgeon Lieutenant Tony Paddon, later a lieutenant-governor of Newfoundland but at the time best known as the destroyer *Skeena*'s doctor; it became a smash hit in the escort navy everywhere. Other groups adopted songs ranging from martial to maudlin, and in some cases individual ships took up some piece of music or other as its own "signature" tune. The corvette *Rimouski* used to enter harbour with her loudspeakers pouring forth the sugary sentiment of "Paper Doll", for reasons known only to herself.

All this cacophony of noise and bravado, of course, was merely the outward evidence of a swelling pride and confidence that transformed Canada's escort groups as they grew in numbers, in equipment, and above all, in training.

Yet always, in Canadian ships, there was a certain insouciance — cockiness, some senior British officers called it, shaking their heads in disapproval — that set them apart from their more staid Royal Navy sisters.

That insouciance was never better illustrated than by the corvette HMCS *Camrose*, en route to take part in the first Allied landings in Africa. As she steamed into the straits, the great shape of Gibraltar loomed to port, grim, enormous, majestic, one of the world's best-known and most impressive landmarks. As *Camrose* steamed past, she was challenged by the signal station on Europa Point.

From Gibraltar: "WHAT SHIP?"

From *Camrose*: "WHAT ROCK?"

INTO BATTLE

CANADA'S MOST IMPORTANT contribution to the defence of freedom was to provide the Allies with two Atlantic ports: Halifax and Sydney. Here, in the easily protected deep-water upper reaches of these two magnificent harbours, were assembled the hundreds of merchant vessels which, loaded with arms and matériel of every sort, were sailed in convoy to transfer strength from America to Britain and, ultimately, to Europe.

The expression of sea power, the end to which all warships and battle fleets are dedicated, is the ability to move one's ships about the oceans as one wishes, and it was this ultimate freedom that the Allies fought to enjoy, the Axis to deny, in the Battle of the Atlantic. Hard and bitter experience had shown that merchantmen faced with long passages across seas infested with enemy submarines could only travel safely in convoys, which were fought through submarine patrol lines by armed escorts of warships. This lesson had to be relearned time and again, and never more painfully than in the First World War, when German U-boats had almost brought Britain to its knees with an all-out campaign against British shipping sailing independently, and had only been beaten by the introduction, in the very nick of time, of the convoy system. It was a lesson driven home yet again by the United States' catastrophic attempt to continue unescorted sailings along its east coast.

But the success of the convoy system was bought at a heavy price. Convoys had to be assembled, ship by ship, over a considerable period of time, until a sufficient number could be collected to make a viable unit. It imposed interminable delays in getting urgently needed supplies to their destination; ships usually spent much more time waiting about for a convoy sailing than at sea. They had also to travel much greater distances than the simple voyage from port to port; they had to be sailed from their port of origin to a convoy assembly port, whence, after frustrating delays, they would be often routed hundreds of miles from the direct route in order to avoid the enemy. For a faster ship, convoy travel meant the wasting of her extra speed in order to plod along at the pace of the slowest vessel, while for a slower ship it often meant sustaining a speed above her economic cruising level in order to keep up, a pace paid for in crew exhaustion and machinery breakdown as well as in added fuel cost. And, once at sea, being in a convoy meant frighteningly close quarters for ships intended for ample sea-room, with anxious officers forced to maintain meticulous station with their enormous and, by naval standards, under-powered vessels, a task made particularly difficult when the ships were empty, riding light in hurricane winds or blinding fog, black night or freezing spray. Collisions could be as damaging as torpedoes, and, to compound the danger, ships had to travel without showing a light or making a sound that might attract an enemy.

In short, travelling in convoy was a costly, dangerous nuisance, but one that had to be borne. And no one knew more about that, or about every aspect of the organization and operation of convoys, than the British. After all, they had been running them for centuries, right back into the early days of sail, and their priceless expertise was put at the disposal of both Canada and the United States from the very beginning of wartime operations on America's Atlantic coast.

When the Admiralty became convinced in 1937 that war with Hitler's Germany was probably inevitable, planning began for the complicated negotiations for imposing state control over private, independent shipping companies, and for the whole complex business of establishing convoy collection ports, ocean routing, and cargo allocation. This enormous undertaking was complete, its staff briefed and its organization in place down to the last typewriter, when war broke out, and the first trade convoy was assembled in Halifax and sailed successfully for overseas. It was under this British organization, gradually taken over by Canadian officers, that Halifax and Sydney became focal points for a convoy system on which the fate of the free world was to depend.

It was to Halifax that fast — eight knots or better — merchantmen made their way from their loading ports, their slower sisters assembling at Sydney, at the easternmost extremity of Nova Scotia's Cape Breton Island. In the early years they proceeded to these ports independently, but after the United States' entry into the war and the subsequent debacle when such shipping was slaughtered by German U-boats, a convoy system was put into force from Cape Cod northward, small groups of ships being shepherded by Canadian escorts from Buzzards Bay and the Cape Cod Canal to Halifax. Ploughing in solemn line ahead through the rural confines of the canal like so many docile cows was an experience a world away from the harsh realities that awaited in the Atlantic, and one that men of the hard-pressed escort groups savoured, especially in wintertime.

All this, the history and background organization of the convoy system, might seem pretty dull stuff; however, the reality of an individual convoy was a good deal more vivid, for each convoy was a separate and distinct enterprise to those taking part in it, a sort of mutual adventure on which we embarked together. You had only to glance at the shipping crowded into Bedford Basin before sailing day to grasp the significance and scope of the operation in which we in the escort groups were about to play a major role.

Bedford Basin, the huge land-locked upper harbour of Halifax, was a closed and separate world during the Battle of the Atlantic, a world given over entirely to merchant shipping. The day after a convoy sailing it was a great grey expanse of empty water, enclosed by a surprisingly rural landscape. The day before a sailing it was crowded with what seemed like every merchant ship in the world, anchored in long lines stretching in every direction, as far as the eye could see. There were ships of every description, of every nationality, for even neutral nations found it safer to sail their ships in convoy than to count on the U-boat's respect for their neutral status. Smartly painted Danes and Swedes mingled with war-worn Britons and salt-stained Greeks, and as the war dragged on an increasing number of American Liberty Ships, fresh from Henry Kaiser's wondrous shipyards, enlivened the rusty ranks of old-timers who'd been at it for years.

Loaded down to their marks and lying deep in the water, they were crammed with every imaginable cargo: supplies to feed, clothe, and minister to the people of besieged Britain, weapons and equipment for their armies, and, above all, oil to fuel the Allied war machine, gasoline for the aircraft, tanks, and motor gunboats fighting Hitler's Germany. Their decks were piled high with cargo too bulky to fit into even the largest hatch, the deepest hold: locomotives and tanks and crated bombers, perhaps. You could tell how the war was going by what these ships were carrying on deck, and it was for this reason that window-blinds were pulled on the seaward side of the passenger cars as the Canadian National Railways' Ocean Limited chuffed its way along the shores of the Basin. You didn't have to be a trained spy to understand that when the ships anchored in the Basin were loaded with landing-craft, the Allies must be planning a seaborne invasion in the near future, and however inadequate the closed blinds were as a security measure, it was at least a gesture that could be appreciated by seamen about to embark on a perilous venture.

Ministering to this vast concourse of shipping were dozens of vessels of every shape and size, ranging from motorboats carrying officials and libertymen from ship to shore, to barges bringing off supplies, tankers topping up fuel bunkers, floating cranes lifting heavy cargo, work-boats effecting repairs. This grubby, harbour-bound armada, and the piers and emergency buildings dotted along the shoreline, were the outward evidence of the enormous and complex organization that had assembled the ships here, would shortly sail them to destinations all over the world, and was even now planning the discharge and onward transport of their cargoes. To even the most insensitive observer, wartime Bedford Basin was a busy and exciting place where the feeling of imminent peril could be felt.

Those ships being degaussed over there were being protected against magnetic mines that might lie in wait; those machine-guns being fitted in the bridge wings of that tanker were in anticipation of aircraft attack; and the big gun being adjusted on the stern of the Liberty Ship was an indication of just what might be encountered on the coming voyage. As sailing day approached, the once-deserted Basin was now packed with shipping, the tension almost tangible, the pace of last-minute repairs and adjustments rising to fever pitch. Sailing day was almost a release, a relief for the thousands of merchant seamen who populated the floating city of Bedford Basin.

You had hardly noticed them in Halifax in their shabby shoreside clothes, quiet men, generally, in their cloth caps and worn raincoats. At their Merchant Seamen's Club in downtown Halifax they played pool, read magazines, wrote letters home to girls or families in Liverpool or London, Piraeus or Bombay. In a city crowded with uniforms, loud with the boisterous tumult of brash young men, they passed unnoticed, on their way to buy "summat for the womenfolk back 'ome"; a little older, a little more reserved, than the servicemen rubbing elbows with them on sidewalks and streetcars. They wore no uniform, but for all that they were the real warriors of the Battle of the Atlantic, and the youngest matelot joining an escort ship on the Triangle Run quickly learned to respect them.

Not that there weren't some aspects of the merchant marine that were the envy of naval escort crews. Pay was vastly higher in merchant ships than in the naval service, and discipline much easier, but, most precious of all, merchant seamen had much more time in port between voyages than their naval counterparts. In the later stages of the war, when warships were plentiful and the escort groups consequently stronger and more numerous, there was time between trips for naval ships to be repaired and maintained, for proper training of ships' companies in sonar, gunnery, and depth-charge drills and of ships' officers in tactical tables and action rooms. But in the spring of 1942, when wave after wave of U-boats was testing the convoy system to its limits, there was time for only the most essential tasks —

taking on fuel, ammunition, food, and water—before an escort ship, still weary and worn from the last convoy, would sail to escort a new one. The few hectic days in port were made even more arduous by the cramped and crowded conditions at the escort berths; it was commonplace for Bangors and corvettes to be nested five and six deep alongside Jetty Five in Halifax or Newfyjohn's South Side, or, even worse, at the trot-buoys in mid-harbour. Simply to maintain the ship became a nightmare for anxious first lieutenants; winter weather meant that the entire ship was constantly being washed down with corrosive salt water while at sea, and trying to paint overside in a snowstorm at the crowded berths was usually impossible, while only the most essential repairs could be handled by the harried dockyard staff. It was commonplace for escorts to be sailed with engine-room defects, with upper-deck damage unrepaired, and short of supplies of one kind or another, with crew shortages remedied, if at all, by a series of last-minute reinforcements or "pierhead jumps" which added a few men, usually right out of cells or training school, to replace key crewmen landed sick or injured.

For Triangle escorts in those terrible months, sailing day arrived all too soon. The convoy conference held the day before departure afforded the most intimate glimpse of the workings of the convoy system. Attended by the captains of all the merchantmen sailing in the new convoy, and by the commanding officers of the escorts under their senior officer, the conference was held, in the early days, in the dining-room of Admiralty House, the Halifax wardroom officers' mess. It was later moved to a featureless conference room in a dockyard office block, but at Ad House the Georgian elegance of plaster mouldings and formal fireplaces imparted a dignified air appropriate to proceedings of considerable consequence.

Just to be a part of a convoy conference was a memorable experience, particularly after the meeting was called to order and the great doors at the end of the room were closed, cutting us off from the outside everyday world, for we in here are bound on a desperate adventure, dark with secrecy and heavy with significance. And while the presiding admiral, his broad bands of gold lace reaching nearly to his elbows, welcomes us with a sort of genial formality, and his staff officers pass out sets of papers to each man seated around the long tables, placed end to end, that fill the room, let us look about us at the faces of the men whose destinies have been brought together around this blue table-top.

Hardly an impressive lot, one might think; their bowlers and fedoras discarded in the hallway, they sit about in their worn, old-fashioned suits, half a hundred middle-aged men puffing cigarettes or adjusting their glasses for the chore of reading through the close-typed lists and papers before them. Few of them wear uniform ashore; their braid and brass buttons, the mark of their seagoing status, is kept for other occasions, for there is no swank about the merchant service. Apart from us escort types, the only gold lace to be seen is at the end of the room under the formal photographs of the King and Queen, where the admiral and his staff are ranged before the fireplace.

A mixed bag: there are pink-faced Englishmen with unfashionable accents — North-countrymen, mostly, with a sprinkling of Cockneys — and dark-eyed, short-assed Welshmen, with the usual leavening of dour Scots, for most of these ships are British. But there are men from other countries here too: a couple of blond Scandinavians conversing together in their outlandish Northern tongue, three surprisingly young Americans, apparently new to the sea, and the inevitable handful of Greeks, sucking at cigarettes, their swarthy faces and drained eyes oppressed with a thousand worries — arrears of pay, crew shortages, antiquated engines, family problems at home.

A little awkward in these elegant surroundings, a little awed by naval pomp and circumstance, it is none the less this haggard huddle of shabby civilians who dominate the room and endow the proceedings with purpose and significance, for these nondescript fellows share a common courage that is one of the wonders of the war. More than the fighter pilots, the commandos, or the dashing torpedo-boat types of our own service, these men truly deserve to be called the Bravest of the Brave.

It is easy to be brave when you are young and ignorant and know that you're going to live forever, but it's different for a middle-aged man with a family, who knows the score, who has watched ships blow up beside him and seen friends die, who knows exactly what horrors may well lie before him on the coming voyage. To go to sea in the face of such knowledge, in a floating bomb loaded with explosives in the hold and high-octane aviation gasoline on deck, takes a kind of cool courage quite beyond our youthful capacity, and we look at these quiet, hard-eyed fellows with a respect that is almost reverence. Yet in a few hours they will become for us the slack lot of wayward incompetents, hell-bent on self-destruction, who must be bullied and cajoled and even shot at if they are ever to be got safely across the ocean as a well-formed convoy.

The admiral fills them in on the world picture, tells them the importance to the war effort of the cargoes they are carrying, wishes them a quick, safe voyage, and then retires to whatever fastness an admiral spends his busy days in, while the specialists take over. A meteorologist, "the met man", tells us what weather to expect, and his predictions produce the usual indulgent disbelief, and an air-force officer tells us what sort of aircraft we can expect to see patrolling over us, and for how long; enough, everyone hopes, to make any U-boats keep their heads down, at least in daylight.

Our own boss takes over then, the escort senior officer, a tough Royal Navy commander and a convoy veteran of long standing. He tells his crowd of merchant skippers what to expect from us and what we're likely to do on encountering an enemy, and what he expects from them in various contingencies. He gets a respectful hearing, but it is the next speaker who captures all eyes and every man's full attention, for this fellow, a peppery, pink-faced old boy with piercing blue eyes and white hair ("You fellows gave me that!") and the thick band of gold lace of a commodore, Royal Navy, is to be convoy commodore, the ruler of all our destinies and our leader in the undertaking on which we are about to embark, and he speaks to us as a shepherd to his flock.

Most of what he says is familiar stuff to many of the skippers, old stagers who've heard it all before a dozen times, but they listen carefully all the same and study the commodore himself, for it is on this man, his abilities and nerve and decision, that our lives and the fate of the convoy itself mostly depend. He is a veteran Royal Navy officer who has come out of retirement to serve again at sea as a convoy commodore. He travels with his own signalling staff in a large merchantman at the head of the convoy, and he is responsible for every aspect of its operation. He consults with authorities ashore and with the escort commander afloat, but it is ultimately he who decides what course to steer, what action to take. When we put to sea, he is the nearest thing to God afloat, and everyone listens as he emphasizes station-keeping, particularly in fog or darkness, a disciplined response to enemy attack, and procedures to be followed by stragglers.

It is obvious in a moment or two that we have landed a good one; we feel confident that we are in safe hands as the conference adjourns and dissolves in a pleasant mixture of coffee and conversation as old friends are recognized and introduced to new, and the international fraternity of the sea strengthens a few more bonds.

Next morning things are not so pleasant. Sailing day begins early, in order to take full advantage of every hour of daylight in forming up the convoy, and at the escort berths we are astir long before dawn. Dim riding-lights glow across the black water, sirens blast briefly as Bangors and corvettes and tugboats sort out the sailing escort from the sleeping tiers of ships alongside, and in the pre-dawn blackness we glide down the harbour in line astern of our leader, an elderly four-stacker. Past the silent dockyard, its great cranes dark shadows above, we steam, our crews busy preparing for sea; past the bulk of the Nova Scotian hotel and the berths where the great liners — the fat-funnelled *Pasteur*, the graceful *Ile de France*, or the magnificent old *Aquitania*, an elegant four-funnelled survivor from a more civilized age — rest briefly between troop-carrying voyages about the world. On the port side, only the vague hump of George's Island passing close aboard and then we are at the gate, the long line of huge floats that support the unseen net stretching into the darkness on either side as we slide into the gap of open water. A shout from the deck of the gate vessel, a clatter of machinery, and we are through to the open sea, and from our destroyer's jagged silhouette an Aldis lamp blinks blearily, ordering us into line abreast ten cables apart and giving us course and speed. We are going to sweep out the harbour approaches ahead of the oncoming convoy, for this funnel-shaped focal point for shipping is a U-boat killing-ground and perhaps the most dangerous place on the whole Triangle Run.

And God knows, any U-boat lurking about has had more than enough warning about our coming. This morning, as on every convoy sailing day, the powerful Halifax commercial radio station has interrupted its usual fare of dance music to blare a stirring rendition of "Rule, Britannia", followed by the announcement: "We have a message for lightkeepers; the message is: 'A for apple, A for apple, is now in effect.' " The message, together with the band music, is repeated three times, as always, in case any tardy lightkeeper — or offshore U-boat — may have missed it initially. It doesn't take any deductive ability to comprehend that lightkeepers on the coast are being told to do something, and since their lights are normally kept dark, this something can only be to turn on all lights and navigation aids. And since lights are only turned on for the convenience of a convoy, the announcement can only mean that a convoy is in the offing, exactly what a U-boat commander needs to know. A German super-spy couldn't have done it better, yet this inane message was broadcast by a government agency for every convoy sailing throughout the war.

In contrast was the heavy-handed official attitude toward convoy secrecy: the warning posters, the darkened train windows, the ridiculous newspaper euphemism "an East Coast port", which could only be Halifax. The mixed signals were probably due, not to treason in high places, as our matelots liked to speculate, but rather to the usual bureaucratic failure, one arm of officialdom not knowing what the other was up to.

And the radio station *did* have its uses. Since its mast was marked on the chart, we were able to get a good bearing on it with our direction-finding radio set. Once, trying to fix our position inward bound, our navigator, tuning in as a popular singer was broadcasting, was heard to call out: "Deanna Durbin's left tit bears 290 degrees magnetic."

Early-rising Haligonians with a view of the harbour were treated to a rare experience on a convoy sailing day. The long line of grey merchantmen filing down-harbour in the wan light of early morning, like so many enormous elephants nose to tail, was a moving, even an awesome, sight. Deep-laden, their decks cumbered with huge crates and clumsy impedimenta of every kind, from wingless aircraft to pontoons or harbour tugs, they moved inexorably past, their latent strength and sense of purpose apparent to the most casual eye. For all that their only armament was an antique gun on the stern and a few light pieces in concrete emplacements scattered about the upper deck, they were more impressive than a battle fleet, their salt-stained flanks the very embodiment of sea power. Every sort of ship was here, from raw new emergency-program Park ships, fresh from a Canadian shipyard, to sea-worn old-timers, familiar in happier days as Blue Funnel, Ellerman, or Bucknall flagships. Alike now in grubby grey, their line was brightened here and there by the bright colours of a neutral-nation ship, still in peacetime livery, with the country's name painted on each side in enormous lettering in the hope it might discourage a German torpedo.

So much for the shoreside observer; to us in the escorts the long line of ships emerging from the harbour entrance represented so many difficult, even refractory, charges, to be chased and chivvied into some sort of proper formation only after a long and exhausting day. Each ship had a position allotted to it carefully chosen by authorities ashore, so that ships breaking off early could depart with minimum disruption, so that those with the most valuable and dangerous cargoes — troopers, tankers, explosives ships — could be tucked in the centre, hopefully shielded by less vulnerable ships on the flanks, and so that column leaders were ships capable of keeping easy station.

Getting them into their proper place in a big convoy — forty ships or more — was a dangerous and exasperating business at best, the big vessels being difficult to manoeuvre at close quarters, and when bad weather caused complications — an onshore gale or the sudden descent of fog — the job became an absolute nightmare. And yet eventually it would be done, and night would fall on a gaggle of ships in some sort of recognizable formation, spread in short columns across a wide front, eight or ten columns, say, each four or at the most five ships deep, for it was the flank, not the front, of a convoy that was most vulnerable to torpedo attack. Cursing, care-worn captains turned their bridges over to watch-keepers and gratefully sought the Spartan comfort of their sea-cabins and the convoy sailed on, already a unit with a name, a commodore, and a sense of identity, to whatever lay in store for it in the darkness ahead.

The Struggle

WHAT LAY AHEAD, of course, was trouble; it was only the degree of trouble that was a matter for conjecture. Trouble could vary from the discomfort of an Atlantic gale and the routine domestic disasters — collisions, breakdowns, sickness, accidental death or injury, and even the occasional suicide — to the all-out devastation wrought by a hurricane or a prolonged mauling by U-boats. Somewhere in between these extremes was the norm for most Triangle runs, but for real trouble you had to sail with a slow convoy out of Sydney, Cape Breton.

The harbour was a fine long affair divided into two arms, with the town itself lying along the southern shore. It always seemed to be raining when we called there, so we never got a really good look at the place, but it seemed a modest little city dominated by an enormous mill that produced vast amounts of smoke and slag and steel and stink, in roughly that order. You could always pick out Sydney from far at sea, long before landfall, by the glow in the sky from the enormous mountains of slag, constantly being refreshed with molten waste.

In the later years of the war a dockyard developed at Point Edward, with a naval bureaucracy to match the naval buildings, as mixed a blessing as one could wish, but in the early days you topped up your bunkers at a greasy old tanker, the *Scottish Musi-*

cian, before berthing at the naval jetty right in front of the town, in the usual pelting rainstorm. Charlotte Street was no Broadway, but there were theatres and shops and restaurants, and our fellows used to slope off ashore happily enough to "size up the local talent". We ourselves never seemed to get past the Isle Royale, a fine big hotel overlooking the harbour, filled with navy friends and navy wives, but we never heard any complaints from the messdecks, and everyone seemed to make themselves at home. ("Are you from the Pier, dear?")

The trouble with Sydney was that, as the sailing port for slow convoys, it was the catch-all for the oldest, rustiest, dirtiest, and most accident-prone set of ships to be found anywhere. They had been hand-picked from the backwaters of every harbour in the globe, for the Allies were desperately short of shipping; if a hulk floated, or could be made, with difficulty, to float, it would be patched up and sent to Sydney to sail in one of the celebrated slow convoys.

Slow was an understatement; snail-like would be closer to the mark. Some of the veterans of the Triangle Run escort groups claimed to have sailed with slow convoys that made seven or eight knots, but six was good going on an Atlantic crossing, and there were plenty of times when four knots was simply whistling along.

Everything was against these rusty antiques, many of them veterans of the First World War or perhaps even of the Boer War. Lying in harbour, with their high, old-fashioned pipe-stem funnels and their general air of dilapidation, they were a sorry enough lot, but to appreciate their true decrepitude one had to see them at sea, their machinery clattering and their ancient structures groaning as they butted into the Atlantic rollers, belch-ing clouds of thick black smoke as their stokers shovelled the

"Sydney Shit", as they scornfully referred to the low-grade Cape Breton coal. Undermanned and underequipped, overloaded and overdriven, these old-timers were cruelly tested by the winter rigours of the North Atlantic, while their slow speed and smoke-making made them especially vulnerable to U-boat attack.

In retrospect, one sees the desperadoes who took these rambling wrecks to sea as the heroes they undoubtedly were, but at the time they seemed to us in the escort ships to be a set of incompetent rascals, forever making smoke, showing lights, straggling or straying out of proper station, and generally making nuisances of themselves.

Signal, from senior officer to corvette: "THE DUCHESS OF RUTLAND IS SHOWING A LIGHT LOW DOWN AMIDSHIPS."

Once ships had found their approximate position in the columns, and had been closed up into tight formation after much signalling from the commodore and a good deal of persuasion from the escorts, life in the convoy settled into an established routine. Every day after the noonday observations of the sun, the commodore would hoist flags indicating the official noon position of the convoy, and he would also signal any course changes as required, usually diversions on account of reported U-boats or, occasionally, the approach of a hurricane.

There were, of course, the usual incidents that might be expected in a floating city of more than a thousand men, embarked in heavily loaded ships with often uncertain and sometimes downright dangerous machinery. It was not unusual for the convoy's only medical doctor, embarked in the senior officer's destroyer, to have to be put on board a merchantman to attend an injured seaman or, if weather permitted, to have a casualty transferred to the destroyer, but usually medical advice could be sent by signal.

From merchantman to destroyer: "PLEASE CAN YOU LET ME HAVE SOME SORT OF MEDICINE FOR SOME SORT OF RASH."

Still, for a destroyer's medical officer who otherwise spent most of his time auditing wardroom bar chits and inspecting the private parts of anxious seamen, a little scramble up the rusty side of a towering merchantman was a welcome break in an otherwise tedious day, especially if the new subby had learned to fight shy of taking him on at gin rummy. Broken limbs and the occasional acute appendicitis, along with burns, cuts, and the usual itches and swellings, made up the routine excitements for Doc; it was only after encounters with the enemy or really bad weather that he could expect to be asked to cope with sterner stuff.

For the rest of us in the escort ships, convoy life had a curiously detached air; we were with it but not of it. We conformed to the convoy's movements, kept station on it, rounded up its stragglers, and succoured its ailing ships and men, but we marched to our own drum, subject to orders from our own senior officer, and to directives from naval authority ashore. We had our own responsibilities, along with the shared obligation for the safe arrival of the ships in convoy, and from our screening positions a mile or so removed, our view of it tended to be surprisingly limited. With the half-dozen escorts available, the senior officer in his destroyer, as the fastest ship, usually stationed himself ahead in the centre, zigzagging back and forth across the broad front of the convoy, with a ship — either corvette or Bangor — level with him wide on each bow. Another escort would be positioned on each side of the convoy and the last — "Tail-end Charlie" — would bring up the rear, zigzagging across the stern of the columns. Distance apart of the escorts varied with asdic operating conditions, the intent being to have the convoy completely screened by overlapping asdic beams. This formation was by no means immutable; in bad weather, when U-boats could be expected to attack only downwind, the senior officer might strengthen the weather side, perhaps even put every ship upwind to intercept the only possible attack route. At other times, often when convoys were being re-formed after an attack or an unusually severe gale, the senior officer might position his destroyer, as the fastest ship, right astern, where all the action was and he was most needed. Whatever your position in the screen, however, your view of the convoy tended to be distinctly parochial; you got to know the appearance, and the characteristics, of the nearest ships very well indeed, the remainder being merely an anonymous mass.

In the days before 271 radar set us all free, we escorts had to keep station visually at night, peering through the rainy or snowy darkness with night glasses for the loom of the nearest ship. Under such conditions, one quickly learned the intimate details of the ships one kept station on, the distinctive masts, booms, ventilators, or funnels that set their silhouettes apart from others. Above all, one soon learned which ships had nervous or impatient captains, who were liable to suddenly pull their ship out of column and head for breathing room to seaward of the convoy. These were the fellows who would come charging at you from out of the blackness, a glimpse of a bow wave or a looming darkness suddenly shutting out a star the only warning of their presence. They added years to the age of every escort watch-keeper. A startled shout from a white-faced lookout, a yelp or a bellow down a voice-pipe, a rapid ringing of telegraph bells, and you usually managed to get your ship out of the way of the oncoming juggernaut, but collisions, and the fear of collisions, were a constant factor on the Triangle Run in the early days.

Tedium was another; convoy escort life was once described as "hours of boredom interrupted by moments of sheer terror". Long stretches of bad weather, with everyone irritated by the constant motion and discomfort and general banging about, could depress the brightest spirit, but the consequent gloom and ennui could be brightened by the practice of sending terse messages from watch-keeper to watch-keeper. Most of these informal exchanges, flashed from a corvette tossing on the outskirts of a convoy to a sister ship only occasionally glimpsed between towering seas, are now long forgotten, but a few were collected by such people as Jack Broome, a famous escort commander, and other gems have lingered on in memory.

December 1941, in Atlantic gale, from bored escort: "COMMENCE HOSTILITIES WITH JAPAN."

From even more bored corvette: "REQUEST PERMISSION TO FINISH BREAKFAST FIRST."

Corvettes, while excellent sea-boats, were extremely lively in bad weather, often standing on their ear when larger ships merely rolled or pitched.

Signal, from one corvette to another: "HAVE JUST SEEN DOWN YOUR FUNNEL. FIRE IS BURNING BRIGHTLY."

And in an escort group hooked on the argot of Damon Runyon, whose Broadway characters were the rage in the early years of the war, the near approach of Newfyjohn might bring a signal to Liverlips from Hot Horse Herbie: "MEET ME AT GOOD TIME CHARLIE'S JOINT [The Crowsnest] WHERE WE WILL INVESTIGATE SOME WET MERCHANDISE."

But the real collector's item, the most enigmatic signal of the war, was the one received by the RCN signal station at Albro Lake for delivery to a seaman aboard a merchant ship in Halifax. Obviously a response to an earlier query, it read: "WHERE-

ABOUTS OF YOUR FATHER UNKNOWN. BELIEVED TO BE TRAVELLING THROUGH EUROPE DISGUISED AS A NUN.''

Tedium, in short, was something that could be lived with; terror was another matter altogether, and on the Triangle Run it could come in a sudden, blinding flash, a shattering explosion in the dark of night.

Submarine torpedo attacks off the Canadian and U.S. seaboard were different from those experienced on the mid-ocean run. Out there, U-boats lay in wait in a series of long patrol lines stretched across the convoy routes. Once contacted, a convoy would become the centre of concerted attacks by ''wolf-packs'' of U-boats, operating almost exclusively at night and usually on the surface, diving only to escape counter-attacking escorts.

On the Canadian seaboard there was little of this wolf-pack business; U-boats were encountered singly or in pairs, and attacks were frequently made by day, by submerged U-boats lying in wait and firing torpedoes, often at a distance, into the mass or ''brown'' of the convoy. There was less selecting of specific targets, even at night; U-boats simply took what was available and then sought escape, often by going deep or, in the shallower waters of the Continental Shelf, by sitting on the bottom until any attack subsided.

The incidence of U-boat attacks varied greatly according to the stage of the war and the success or failure U-boats were experiencing elsewhere. There were stretches of months at a time when not a single submarine would be sighted on the Triangle Run, to be followed by periods of intense U-boat activity. In Canadian waters, most U-boats encountered were on passage, fresh from port and with full loads of torpedoes, fuel, and food, on their way to the happy hunting-grounds to the south, off the U.S. seaboard. This was particularly so in the spring and summer of 1942, when the prospect of sinking unescorted American ships like shooting fish in a barrel drew swarms of U-boats to the western Atlantic. On their way south the U-boats traversed Canadian waters, and their numbers and ferocity tested the convoy escorts to their very limits.

These were the terrible days on the Triangle Run, an ordeal in which the inadequate numbers and equipment of Canadian escorts were reflected in heavy losses of merchantmen under escort. At the same time, the value of even such limited protection was dramatically illustrated by contrasting convoy sinkings, however heavy, with the simply staggering losses of unescorted shipping to the south. In 1942 the convoy system came of age, and from the hard-won experience of Canada's escort groups came both the expertise and the equipment that would turn the Battle of the Atlantic around, and give escorts the upper hand over the U-boat.

More ships, better armed and equipped, with bigger and better-trained crews and operating tactically as a cohesive unit, cut the number of merchantmen losses with each passing month, and at the same time increased the number of U-boats sunk. Yet the threat of submarine attack was always there, right to the last; in December of 1944 a new Liberty Ship was torpedoed and sunk right in the Halifax approaches while a convoy was being formed up, and three days later, on Christmas Eve, in the same waters, the Bangor HMCS *Clayoquot* was also torpedoed.

It was a particularly grisly sinking. *Clayoquot* was one of a number of escorts sent out to hunt for *U-806*, which had finally managed to sink the SS *Samtucky* off Sambro after bumbling about making poor attacks with faulty torpedoes, and which fired an acoustic torpedo as it dived to avoid the oncoming Bangor. The resulting explosion blew *Clayoquot*'s stern section right up into the air, where it poised at a ninety-degree angle high above the rest of the quarterdeck, trapping two officers in their cabin below. In the frantic seconds that followed as crewmen abandoned their rapidly sinking ship in an urgent but orderly manner, *Clayoquot*'s company, officers and men alike, had to endure the pleas and entreaties of their trapped shipmates as the two desperate officers, Lieutenant Paul Finlay (n) and Sub-lieutenant William Munro, alternately thrust their bleeding heads through their cabin scuttle, a porthole too small to permit escape. Both were RCNVR officers, Munro having joined fresh from his initial officers' training school and Finlay, an experienced officer, after completion of his specialized navigation course. The explosion had sealed off all access to them and to any tools that might have been used to help free them; in an agony of horror and frustration, *Clayoquot*'s survivors watched helplessly as their two young officers were borne screaming into the dark depths.

It was a terrible ending to a traumatic experience, made even ghastlier by the final explosion of *Clayoquot*'s ready-use depth-charges as the sinking vessel reached their fifty-foot setting, and the wretched survivors, clinging to their rafts in the numbing cold, were overwhelmed by the tragedy. But their spirits rose to the occasion; one of them, the irrepressible Coder Alex Batt of Islington, Ontario, raised a grin with a shouted imitation of the typical Canadian radio news flash, which always depicted every wartime event as a Canadian triumph: "Flash! Canadian Minesweeper Destroys German Torpedo!" Only a Canadian sailor, and a volunteer "wavy-navy" reservist at that, could have responded in such a fashion in such a situation.

Indeed, it was this wry, irreverent, self-deprecating humour that, more than anything else, set Canadian seamen apart from our German U-boat contemporaries. We shared the same miserable conditions and had a grudging respect for some of the more capable commanders, although there was nothing very impressive about the few shivering survivors we had hauled aboard from a sunken submarine, the only members of the "Master Race" we had ever seen. On the other hand, no Allied seaman could ever stomach the arrogant posturing of the U-boat men that we watched in movie newsreels: the brass bands, the vainglorious songs, the strutting admirals, the buxom maidens draping garlands of flowers about the necks of their returning warriors. Only a Nazi could transform the sinking of helpless merchant ships and the drowning of their unarmed sailors into Wagnerian heroics. Certainly we had no such illusions, and when one U-boat survivor attempted an arrogant, arm-in-the-air Nazi salute upon being hauled aboard a Canadian corvette, he was unceremoniously bundled back overside to rethink the situation.

The same arrogance was displayed in U-boat log-books, as postwar historians were to discover. References to the Führer and the Fatherland, and patriotic exhortations and lip-smacking ("We will teach the Yankees a lesson!") in what were supposed to be operational records, strike a jarring note in Canadian ears accustomed to the laconic, unemotional style learned from the Royal Navy. And for all their jingoistic fervour, the truth was that U-boat performance in Canadian waters was very indifferent, a series of ill-coordinated and misdirected attacks without any overall plan or purpose. A few commanders — the redoubtable Hartwig in particular — displayed remarkable individual aggressiveness and tenacity, but their attacks were hit-or-miss affairs on ships they seem to have stumbled upon, rather than the sustained, co-ordinated affairs mounted against mid-ocean convoys. For a people that prided itself on mechanical precision, the abysmal performance of German torpedoes is hard to explain, for throughout the war they accounted for more misses than hits.

But above all it was German thick-headedness that impresses Canadian escort seamen in retrospect, a lack of awareness that exceeded even the fabled insensitivity of our own beloved NSHQ. Germans seemed unaware that Canada was a country separate from the United States, and classed us all as "Yankees". Right to the end of the war, U-boat commanders seemed unaware of long-established trade routes, of escort and assembly ports, of seasonal trade patterns and well-established ferry routes. Their inability to distinguish between classes of warships and aircraft seems amazing in men whose lives might well depend on instant recognition of an approaching enemy.

One of the most surprising aspects of German naval operations against Canada was the failure to mount any sustained mining effort against a country peculiarly susceptible to such operations. From the first, Ottawa had been worried about the vulnerability of Halifax approaches and the St. Lawrence estuary to mining, and as a result not only had built scores of Bangor and Algerine minesweepers but had fitted all its early corvettes with minesweeping gear. As it happened, only a handful of trawler-type sweepers and a few wooden-hulled vessels had been required to keep these waters clear. A couple of U-boats had laid a few mines here and there off Halifax and St. John's, in hopeful fashion, and these had claimed a coaster or two, but it had been done in such a slapdash manner that most of the mines, of the moored contact type, broke surface and bobbed about at the end of too-long moorings.

It was one of these that provided Newfoundlanders, notoriously fond of tall tales, with one of their best stories of the war. A fisherman, Llewellyn Curtis, came across a floating German mine that had broken away from its anchor off the northeast coast of Newfoundland in the summer of 1941. Unaware of what it was, and anxious to make use of the steel wire he could see trailing from it as a mooring pendant for his boat, he put a line on the strange "buoy" with its projecting horns and towed it back to his home port in La Scie Harbour, Cape St. John. With the help of some neighbours, he removed the wire he wanted and then, unwilling to discard such an unusual object, they hoisted it onto the pier and rolled it along to Curtis's shed.

For the next couple of weeks Curtis and his wonderful "booey" were the talk of the town; people came to peer inside the strange contrivance and marvel at its elaborate mysteries. The eight big horns, for instance: Curtis unbolted them, one by one, and displayed them proudly on his workbench. For his admiring neighbours, Curtis would unscrew a central bolt, allowing a "trapdoor" to open and reveal the wonders within; wires of different colours and batteries in there, "snug and dry and good as new".

Eventually an appalled police constable heard of the find and removed it into official keeping, but not before Llewellyn Curtis and his wonderful "booey" had passed into Newfy legend.

So much for the German mining effort. But for sustained low comedy, nothing could equal the cloak-and-dagger buffoonery of the two "intelligence missions" mounted by German U-boats against Canada.

In May 1942 a U-boat, *U-213*, after blundering about the Bay of Fundy with out-of-date charts, landed an agent, Langbein-Haskins, on the shore near Saint John, New Brunswick, whence he made his way by road and train to Montreal. Plagued by the out-of-date currency supplied him (a wad of $20 bills issued in 1917 and taken from some Canadian soldier in the First World

War), Langbein-Haskins had to find some refuge where his money might be accepted without any questions asked. He shacked up in a series of brothels in Montreal and Ottawa, where he lived the good life until his money ran out. Penniless and ill, he gave himself up to the Naval Intelligence Directorate in 1944, having contributed absolutely nothing to his Fatherland's war effort.

Despite this discouraging adventure, German intelligence tried yet again. In the fall of 1942, *U-518* landed 41-year-old Werner von Janowski, a former immigrant to Canada who had worked as a farm labourer in Ontario, on the beach near New Carlisle on the Baie des Chaleurs. Here he buried his naval officer's uniform, which would prove him a combatant and not a spy in the event of his capture, before setting off in the growing light of dawn for the nearby town.

He was outfitted for his cloak-and-dagger mission in the best Katzenjammer Kids tradition, with an enormously heavy wireless transmitter, packed into a big suitcase, and a strange briefcase, obviously made in Germany, containing one thousand dollars in U.S. twenty-dollar gold coins — not the easiest thing to pass in wartime Canada! — and wads of the outsize Canadian bills issued in 1917, together with a small amount of Canadian currency of more recent date. Along with this were the tools of his trade: secret writing materials, an automatic pistol, a set of spiked brass knuckles, some emergency rations, street maps of several Canadian cities, and a Canadian registration card which proclaimed him to be William Branton, of 323 Danforth Avenue, Toronto. To add verisimilitude, he was provided with an English-language novel. It was *Mary Poppins* — just what an ordinary Canadian businessman might be expected to read.

Everything about this strange figure dragging his suitcase along a Canadian highway in the grey Canadian dawn shrieked "Foreigner!". His clothes, his demeanour, his luggage were all odd to a Canadian eye, and, worst of all, he stank to high heaven after weeks of being cooped up in a notoriously smelly U-boat. All that was needed to complete the comic-strip caricature was a label pinned to his coat: "Spy".

Janowski checked into the little hotel in New Carlisle to revel in a bath and try and rid himself of the rank U-boat stench, and inevitably he aroused the suspicions of the hotel-keeper. The police were notified and Janowski, after being handed on by them to the RCMP, cheerfully agreed to their proposal to become a double agent. For the rest of the war he fed "doctored" information to his "control" in Germany, via a Canadian transmitter furnished by the Mounties; his own Telefunken in its heavy suitcase lacked the range to reach Germany. So much for the suave Nazi agent, omniscient and diabolically clever, of wartime Hollywood legend!

But the real knockabout comedy act was the Great Escape of 1943, a legend in wartime Canadian wardrooms and messdecks, and still fondly recalled at naval reunions. In the summer of 1943 Canadian intelligence, using the well-established code-crackers, had learned of German plans to organize a mass break-out of U-boat prisoners, led by former ace Otto Kretschmer, from the prisoner-of-war camp at Bowmanville, Ontario. Once the Kretschmer party had tunnelled out of the camp and made its way to the St. Lawrence shore, it would be taken off by U-boat and borne back to a welcoming Fatherland, so the plan went, and in due course *U-536* was dispatched with orders to patrol in the Gulf of St. Lawrence and arrive off Pointe de Maisonnette no later than September 26, 1943.

But back in Bowmanville, everything had gone wrong for the German escapers. The RCMP had discovered money, maps, and other material to be used in the attempt, hidden in the covers of books sent from Germany through the Red Cross, had photographed them, and then allowed them to be delivered in the camp.

The Mounties now became co-conspirators in the planned breakout, their sole aim being to ensure that nothing went wrong in these early stages that would prevent the prisoners from rendezvousing with the U-boat the Canadians hoped to capture. A blind eye was turned by prison guards to any evidence of covert activity by the prisoners; a little subsidence here, a bit of fresh earth there, curious bumping noises in the night. What tunnel?

There was a small contretemps when the radio receiver the prisoners were allowed, which they hoped to convert into a transmitter for use in contacting the U-boat, was found to be too weak for the job. The Mounties promptly managed to have a more powerful radio tube "accidentally" left in the camp where the prisoners could find it; another hurdle surmounted!

Alas, the mass breakout was never made; the great tunnel, now more than three hundred feet long, was never used, although it reached out beyond the camp perimeter wire. Perhaps the Mounties were too helpful, the blind eye too obvious. In any event, the prisoners smelled a rat and the whole caper was called off, with no one more disappointed than the RCMP. But their chagrin was compounded when a single prisoner, Wolfgang Heyda, former captain of *U-434*, took advantage of the planned U-boat pick-up attempt and made a daring solitary breakout on his own. Armed with the prisoners' map and other information, he made himself a set of climbing irons and climbed the tall pole that stood inside the camp and rode on a homemade bosun's chair along the camp power line to the big pole outside, down which he escaped. Catching everyone off guard, he made his escape in the dead of night, and set off on his daring attempt to rendezvous with the expected U-boat.

Armed with a Canadian registration card that showed him to be Fred Thomlinson of 46 Cogswell Street, Toronto, he was dressed in the uniform of a Canadian army sergeant, and had no difficulty in travelling by train to Bathurst, New Brunswick, subsequently arriving on foot at the rendezvous point at Pointe de Maisonnette, where he camped on the beach and awaited developments.

Meanwhile, the navy had been called in to entrap the anticipated U-boat, and it set about its appointed task with gleeful zest. With the connivance of the Commander in Chief, Atlantic, and Captain (D), Halifax, a motley force consisting of the ancient RN destroyer *Chelsea*, three corvettes (HMCS *Agassiz*, *Lethbridge*, and *Shawinigan*), five Bangors (HMCS *Granby*, *Chedabucto*, *Mahone*, *Swift Current*, and *Ungava*), and a number of Fairmiles, was made available for the operation, backed up by the Canadian navy's "secret weapon", HMCS *Rimouski*. Fondly referred to as "the Polish corvette", because of her name, this ship was experimenting with "silhouette lighting", in which a row of lights, controlled by a photo-electric cell, illumined her outline to match the light in her background, thus rendering her practically invisible. Commanded by Lieutenant Jack "Pick" Pickford, RCNVR, she was intended to come to close quarters when the U-boat was sighted.

Lieutenant-Commander Desmond "Debbie" Piers, RCN, was in charge of the operation, and he assembled a staff that included a Royal Navy submariner, Lieutenant "Rocky" Hill, and a naval intelligence officer, Lieutenant-Commander Sorenson, who spoke fluent German. On the appointed night, with his eager flotilla tucked away out of sight behind a headland, a couple of mobile radar units set up overlooking the bay, and his soldier sentries deployed around the point, Piers emulated a famous naval forebear, Sir Francis Drake, on a similar occasion and retired to play a game, not of bowls, but of bridge with his staff in the adjacent lighthouse building on Pointe de Maisonnette.

The game was scarcely under way when it was interrupted by the appearance of Heyda, who had been picked up and arrested by army sentries on their first patrol along the beach. He was handed over to the RCMP and returned to store in Bowmanville, while Piers and his crew set about the chancy business of entrapping the expected U-boat.

It duly turned up, on schedule: *U-536*, commanded by Rolf Schauenburg, already understandably jittery. He had distrusted the whole mission from the start, and a glimpse of Piers's distant ships on the way into the bay had done nothing to reassure him. He was further alarmed when radio messages were received from the shore on a different frequency from the one the escapees were supposed to be using, on a set they had put together in camp, and the code-word used was not according to plan. But the real capper was the signal made from shore by flashing light, the single word "Komm!"

It was just what the spider might have said to the fly in the celebrated nursery rhyme, and for the jumpy Schauenburg, already sensing the shadowy ships sealing off the bay behind him, it was the last straw. Aborting the mission, he now concerned himself entirely with extricating his U-boat from a decidedly sticky situation, and he did it in a notably bold — and successful — manner. Realizing that the surface ships would be expecting him in deep water, he took *U-536* right into the shallows close to shore and made his way around, bumping over the Miscou Flats, in water barely deep enough to cover the boat, and away out of the bay, leaving his frustrated attackers milling about in a welter of false echoes and exasperation.

The whole thing was the kind of hilarious balls-up that naval veterans dearly cherish, and it is generally agreed that the sending of the signal "Komm!" was an especially delicious touch, worthy of a Three Stooges comedy at its worst. These distractions apart, German submarines, manned by tenacious and tough commanders and crews, were a constant source of concern in Canadian waters throughout the war, despite fluctuations in the number and intensity of attacks.

Yet for all the predations of U-boats, it was weather that was the principal enemy on the Triangle Run. The weather experienced off the Canadian Atlantic coast was worse than anything known in mid-ocean or in British home waters, and it is the terrible weather—the monumental storms, the biting blizzards—that lives on in the memory of everyone who served at sea in Canada's winter convoys.

Giant seas, whipped up by hurricane winds in mid-ocean, rose to terrifying heights and crested in flying foam as they reached the shallower waters of the Continental Shelf, and could simply engulf any vessel caught beam-on. And when the biting cold of a Canadian winter added blinding snow and freezing spray to such winds, they smashed whole convoys apart, huge merchant ships driving helplessly before them, to capsize from the weight of ice on their topsides or smash into the breakers of a rockbound shore.

Life in the escort ships, always miserable in a blow, under such conditions became almost past endurance. Ice built up on guns, bridge-houses, masts, ventilators, everything that projected above deck and was exposed to the freezing spray. First only a few inches of a glass-like covering, it quickly grew into foot-thick coatings of rock-hard ice; tons upon tons of it. Desperate seamen hacked at it with fire-axes, crowbars, hammers, anything that could dislodge a few hundredweight of the gleaming white menace that was dragging their ship down. As the terrible topweight grew, the ship's movements became sluggish, her rolling ever heavier, her listings more prolonged, her recovery ever slower. In a nightmare of frenzied fighting, arm-weary ships' companies strove to keep their ship afloat and themselves alive.

Icing was the particular problem of westbound convoys. Prevailing winds were westerly, and freezing spray only became a danger as the ships gradually left the moderating influence of mid-ocean and approached the American continent, where wintertime meant intense cold, and snow could be expected as a regular condition. Westbound convoys were made up of ships in ballast, for the U.K. could export only a fraction of the huge amounts of imports necessary to sustain the Allied war effort, and these ships, riding high and exposing vast areas to wind and spray, were especially vulnerable to icing conditions. As the temperature dropped, hour by hour, the build-up of ice began, and in a westerly gale capsizing became a real threat for even the largest merchantmen.

For low-lying escort ships, especially destroyers with their narrow hulls and extensive top-hamper, severe icing was commonplace in even relatively light winds, and such ships regularly berthed in Halifax encased in thick ice from waterline to yard-arm.

Adding to the hardship imposed by bad weather on naval vessels was the exposed position of watch-keepers on bridges open to the sky. It was essential for officers of the watch to have an unobstructed view in all directions, especially in pre-radar days when a visual outlook was the only method of establishing the position of ships in the vicinity; if you couldn't see it, it would probably run into you. As a consequence, destroyer and corvette bridges were sheltered only by shoulder-high dodgers of canvas or steel, and even the Bangors built flimsy little wooden "monkey-islands" atop their closed bridges in order to improve visibility when escorting convoys. You got a wonderful view of things from these airy playpens, but they were a mite draughty at the best of times and downright miserable in a blizzard or a hurricane.

Hurricanes were another *specialité de la maison* off the American coast. From late summer through the fall — "July, stand by; October, all over" was an old seaman's adage — great tropical storms would move up the east coast from their spawning-ground in the Caribbean, and then swirl off northeastwards from Cape Hatteras, often cutting right across the established convoy routes. For seamen in the escort ships, with a freeboard of only a couple of feet above the waterline, the monstrous seas and incredible winds of a hurricane were a terrifying ordeal, and they made the close quarters of a convoy impossible for even the largest merchantmen.

A hazard affecting the Newfoundland corner of the infamous Triangle was the seasonal migration of icebergs. From late spring through midsummer enormous icebergs would drift down the eastern shores of Labrador and Newfoundland, moving slowly but inexorably southward to their extinction through melting in the warmer temperatures of the south Atlantic. Even radar could be undependable at times in detecting ice, which for some reason often failed to register much of a "blip" on a radar screen, and it could be absolutely shattering on a dark night to suddenly find oneself a scant few yards away from something as tall as a skyscraper and roughly the area of Dauphin, Manitoba, peopled with more seabirds and seals than one could find in a well-stocked zoo. And if bergs could make things a bit dodgy east of Cape Race on a black night, they could be an absolute hell in fog.

Fog. Thick, wet, impenetrable fog, shutting out any glimpse of the world beyond one's fo'c'sle, and then filling it with a thousand noises, real and fancied. "There! Broad on the port bow; did you hear it? Listen — sounded just like surf breaking." (Or a whistle, or a bow-wave; take your pick.) On hundreds of ships, especially before radar lightened the load a bit, watch-keepers craned their necks and cupped their ears to a myriad of perils, mostly illusory but occasionally real, and in convoy they kept rigid station on fog buoys streamed from the stern of each ship, a cask or some other contrivance which, when towed at the end of a line, made a disturbance in the water. The strain of keeping station in thick weather must have measurably shortened the lives of merchant-ship officers, and out on the convoy flanks it etched lines of fatigue and stress on the faces of even the youngest and most feckless escort captains.

More than anything else, fog was part of the way of life on the eastern seaboard, which embraced some of the most fog-prone areas in all the world. It could come at any time, but it was particularly bad on the Grand Banks in early spring and off Nova Scotia and New England in summertime, and it made life afloat dangerous anywhere. Harbours could be worse than the open sea in fog, with tiers of ships anchored in midstream, ringing bells to warn off convoys filing inbound or groping their way seaward, their whistles growling a warning at regular intervals. Altogether a hairy business, fog; a fellow could get into a lot of trouble just shifting berth from Halifax dockyard to the French Cable wharf on the other side of the harbour. ("Steer east until you run into something; you can't miss it.")

Fog compounded every problem, added danger to every sticky situation. Fog and an oncoming convoy; fog and icebergs; fog and a U-boat attack; fog just as a convoy was forming up; most of the nightmares that still plague the aging veterans of the Triangle Run involve fog.

The strain imposed by fog, and the physical battering inflicted by constant bad weather, drained the energy and vitality of even the hardiest, particularly in the early years when escorts were few in number and poorly equipped. The shortage of ships often meant that an escort arriving in port with one group would be fuelled and supplied with all dispatch and sent off with a departing group to fill in for some ship unable to sail because of mechanical defects. On arrival at that group's destination, she might well be dispatched as escort for some local convoy en route to rejoin her own lot. The Naval Officers in Charge at small ports scattered around the coast dearly loved to have a visiting ship from another command at their disposal, to be sent off to escort some dredge or scow in place of their own local ships.

Always it was the most junior ship of the group that would be sent on these gruelling rounds, and as we always seemed to be more junior than anyone, we invariably drew the short straw.

Once we went for thirty-one days, usually in sight of land, without ever being able to enjoy a night in harbour. The mental and physical exhaustion from such a ceaseless round was utterly demoralizing; one longed for a respite, any respite, from the continual buffeting and the endless strain. Hove to in a force 8 gale off Scatarie Island one snowy evening, we caught a glimpse of the lighthouse there and instantly we could picture the keeper and his family, sitting down to dinner in their snug little house, with the prospect of a quiet evening and a peaceful night in warm, dry beds ahead of them. Worn and bruised and soaked through, ducking down behind the dodger when we shipped a sea green over the fo'c'sle, we looked with longing at the distant lighthouse cottage, and would have given anything to enjoy its peace and comfort.

But of course, once in port it was all forgotten, and one swaggered about as a seagoing sailor.

For some reason it is the incidental rather than the routine that is remembered when old sailors recall life on the Triangle Run: the botched, the comic, the fouled-up, the bizarre. Such as when the corvette *Trail*, arriving in harbour right after Christmas, was informed that she was too late to share in the base's Christmas turkeys; the last had been given to the corvette alongside her, which had arrived the previous day. Stung by this injustice, two of *Trail*'s seamen raided their sleeping sister ship in the dead of night, one holding the other by the ankles while he hung upside down from the galley skylight and scoffed four of the birds intended for the other ship's dinner. Each stuffing a pair of birds under his duffle-coat, the two rascals were heading for their ship when they heard the approaching footsteps of what must be an aroused — and armed — quartermaster going his rounds. Deciding to brazen it out, the thieves assumed a nonchalant composure as the stranger approached them, but as each became aware of the ridiculous figure they cut with their swollen chests — like a pair of nursing mothers out for a midnight stroll — their nerve broke in a fit of giggles and, rushing to the side, they dumped the turkeys from under their coats into the harbour. Their chagrin when the approaching stranger turned out to be, not a hostile quartermaster but a fellow *Trail* seaman returning late from ashore, was not eased by the sad spectacle of the four turkeys, white in the pale starlight, sailing serenely off into the blackness astern on the flooding tide.

There is a curiously rueful aspect to nostalgia; how often it seems to be the domestic disaster, rather than the triumph, that comes to mind in recalling the past. The humiliation of having to be taken in tow after an engine failure or perhaps a wire around the screw, and to have to endure the patronizing condescension of the helper towards the helped, is something not easily forgotten, nor is the British signal that exemplified that condescension, made by the tow-er to the tow-ee as the towline was being passed: "TAKE MUMMY'S HAND."

But there were dreadful incidents too, happenings too tragic to dwell on. Like the foggy morning off the Newfoundland coast when the Bangor HMCS *Georgian*, out on the wing of a convoy, caught sight of a surfaced submarine in the swirling mists. Quickly challenging by signal lamp and receiving no reply, she immediately rammed and sank the intruder, only to learn that her victim, lost with all hands, was the British submarine *P-514*. In bad visibility and with no radar, the submarine had strayed from her surface escort for a brief hour while en route to training exercises off St. John's. Her failure to respond when challenged — a faulty lamp, perhaps, or an inattentive signalman? — remains a mystery, but the snuffing out of all those young lives was a tragedy that haunted *Georgian* and her fellow escorts for a long time, even after *Georgian* blew a German U-boat to the surface with a well-placed pattern of depth-charges a few months later, right in the approaches of Sydney harbour.

The bizarre, the macabre, incidents also live on in memory. There was the weird encounter off Long Island Sound experienced by the corvette HMCS *Drumheller* and the destroyer HMS *Montgomery*, one of the Royal Navy's four-stackers, during a depth-charge attack on what appeared to be a U-boat sitting on the bottom in shallow water. Following on after a good attack by *Drumheller*, which had dropped an accurate ten-charge pattern on a rock-solid asdic echo, *Montgomery* was making her run-in when an incredible thing happened. Suddenly, from out of the water ahead of them, the destroyer's officers were appalled to see a huge wall, a darker black against the night sky, protruding upward as an enormous object rose from the depths, so close that collision seemed unavoidable. This fearful apparition from the deep rose up, up, even as *Montgomery* swerved violently, under full helm, to avoid it. There was a roaring of water, a fearful stink, and a terrific clang as *Montgomery*'s stern collided with what could only be heavy steel plating, and then, dim against the skyline, the destroyer's officers could just make out the mast, superstructure, and squat funnel of a merchant ship, seeming immense at such close quarters. Like some fearful monster of myth, rising from its lair at the bottom of the sea, the apparition towered over the stunned onlookers before, with a long, sobbing sigh of escaping air, it sank once more beneath the black waters of the Sound.

It was some time before the shaken officers on the bridges of destroyer and corvette were able to conclude that their exploding depth-charges had upset the distribution of air in a sunken wreck, causing it to rise to the surface momentarily before once again returning to its disturbed resting place on the sea bottom.

Sometimes it was a small, a trivial, incident that lived on in memory, a touch of pathos that could flood the heart with pity. A photograph — a girl? A child? It was too far to see — glimpsed in the grey light of early morning amid flotsam and oily muck where a ship had been sunk the night before. The lover, the father who had treasured that picture, had he drowned or survived? Who could tell?

A wooden raft encountered off the Banks on a misty morning, adrift on an oily sea, its only occupant a small black-and-white dog staring with sightless eyes as we swept past. Only a mongrel, the pet of some sailor, no doubt, in a merchantman torpedoed somewhere far to the south, but to men inured to the site of the dead and dying, that huddled heap of fur was strangely moving. More than a dog, more than a pet, it was innocence that had been done to death here, and the reality of war seemed suddenly harsh and cruel.

Yet of all the encounters at sea that were part of the experience of everyone on the Triangle Run, perhaps none better exemplified the horror and heroism of the wartime Atlantic than that of the veteran destroyer HMS *Montgomery*.

She had come upon it unexpectedly, on a snowy January morning south of Cape Race, a solitary lifeboat with six occupants sitting upright in the thwarts. There had been no movement, no shout or sound of any kind, as Roger Puxley brought his old ship gently alongside, and it was only when a couple of the destroyer's crewmen jumped aboard that the lifeboat could be secured.

In addition to the six men still sitting motionless in their seats, *Montgomery*'s sailors, staring down into the boat, could now see that there were a further six men lying on the bottom boards, but a closer look showed that they were dead, covered with ice from freezing spray. The remaining six, though still alive, were in little better condition. All were frost-bitten; some were frozen to the thwarts on which they sat. But one in particular drew horrified gasps from the onlookers. He had managed to clothe himself only with a short coat; from the waist down he was naked, his lower torso and legs black as coal and covered with a thin sheet of ice — and yet he lived, his eyes rolling upward in mute appeal.

Sitting in the stern sheets, his hand frozen around the tiller, sat a giant of a man, his physique and position at the helm showing that it was he who was in command of this crew of the dead and the dying. He alone was still capable of speech, and as *Montgomery*'s crewmen reached out helping hands, it was he who instructed them to remove the others of his crew first.

One by one they were freed from their frozen perches, lifted carefully up to the destroyer's rail, and then borne in strong arms down to the warmth of the wardroom flat, where they were laid on mattresses with a tender solicitude surprising in such a company. The last to be carried aboard was the big helmsman; as he was borne up the boat was cast loose, to bear its cargo of frozen dead to some final resting place beneath the waves.

Down in the wardroom, the clothing of the survivors was cut away, and they were wrapped, as gently as possible, in warm blankets, while the ship's doctor gave each an injection of pain-killing morphine. All but the helmsman, that is; waving away the doctor and his needle, the big man asked to see the destroyer's captain; until he spoke to him, he said, he would accept no pain-killer, lest he die in his sleep and his story die with him.

Commander Puxley, his lean face pink from the icy wind of his exposed bridge, knelt beside the grey-faced form wrapped in a blanket and listened to the tale he told.

His name was Larsen, the survivor whispered. He had been bosun of the SS *Friar Rock*, a merchantman that had been delayed and missed its convoy sailing date and had then sailed alone in an attempt to catch up with its convoy. Like many stragglers, it had been intercepted and sunk by a U-boat, *U-130*, and thirty-eight survivors had crowded into two lifeboats. In mountainous seas, one boat disappeared; the other had drifted in blizzard conditions for four days, the driving spray and freezing temperatures quickly sapping the life from men dressed only in the clothes they had been wearing when their ship was struck. They died, and froze, where they sat or lay.

At first the bodies had been pushed overside, Larsen said, but as the living dwindled in numbers and strength they had been unable to continue to do so, and the last six had been left to lie where they had died. Larsen had steered the boat downwind in an attempt to avoid the worst of the driving, freezing spray and had sat at the tiller throughout four long days and nights. His responsibility ended, his story told, the burly bosun gratefully accepted the doctor's relaxing injection and drifted peacefully off to sleep.

Throughout the long day and night that followed as the destroyer raced for Halifax, *Montgomery*'s men fought for the lives of their half-dozen waifs. They had been plied with neat rum, bringing animation back to lustreless eyes, but with returning circulation they suffered agonies in their frozen limbs. Worst of all had been the frightful sufferings of the man with the frost-blackened body; his agony had been such that he had to be kept under almost total sedation.

Having arrived in Halifax, *Montgomery* had surrendered her survivors anxiously to the fleet of ambulances that waited alongside; at the end of the working day her libertymen had trooped off to hospital to learn how "their" patients were doing.

The frost-blackened man had been the first to go; he had been hopelessly frozen, and he died within hours of entering hospital.

One by one the others had been taken to the operating room;

first this limb, then that, had been diagnosed as gangrenous and had been amputated. One by one the damaged limbs had been removed for the sake of the healthy trunks, until at last all five survivors, including Larsen, the giant bosun, and a Canadian, Mac Wilson of Forest, Ontario, were double amputees.

Of a ship's company of thirty-eight, there were only these five survivors, and not one leg left among them.

In the North Atlantic winter, life could sometimes be crueller than death.

Charades

THROUGHOUT THE COURSE of the Second World War, the actual fighting along the convoy routes and off distant shores was supplemented by a curious kind of "shadow war", a sort of charade, carried out with all the outward semblance and mimic fury of the real thing, but accepted by all who took part in it as a kind of game, to be played out in mock seriousness but signifying nothing. The ships taking part in this make-believe war were a motley collection of former yachts, tugboats, elderly government steamers, and miscellaneous motor launches, and they were engaged in the defence of Canada's coasts through patrols and the conducting, off every ocean harbour, of an examination service, which, in theory at least, stopped and checked the credentials of every ship before allowing it to enter.

This ragtail fleet was a sort of purgatory which most naval personnel had to endure before experiencing real navy life, particularly in the early years when much of the strength of the Royal Canadian Navy was made up of such improvised warships. It was particularly frustrating for keen young types, thirsting for action on the high seas, to be posted to some grey-painted cockleshell named *Nitinat* or *Ambler* and assigned a berth alongside the ammunition lighter or the harbour dredger. If he was lucky he might find himself aboard some former millionaire's yacht large enough to sport a popgun on her forward deck — an old Hotchkiss from the Boer War, say, or even an elderly twelve-pounder bequeathed from some Victorian coal-burner. Or he could end up on the Pacific coast, as we did, aboard a gasoline-powered motorboat whose only offensive weapon was her captain's ferocious vocabulary, acquired after years in tow-boats, backed up by the fire-power of a stripped Lewis machine-gun.

The firing of this weapon, carried out only under the most stringent conditions (no ships or any sign of life as we know it within sight), was attended by all the martial ritual and meticulous attention to the minutiae of procedure observed in the battle cruiser *Hood* when she was firing her main armament, and was watched, with suitable reverence and from a respectful distance, by all twelve of our ship's company, including the cook and the motor mechanic supposedly tending our engines. As the gunner and his mate, suitably solemn, went about the fearful business of readying the weapon, pulling cocking levers and affixing ammunition pans and so on, calling out in a clear voice just what they had done, everyone was made aware that we were dealing here with a LETHAL WEAPON.

And, sure enough, after the gunner had called out, in the mandatory loud gunnery voice, "Permission to open fire, sir?" and the captain had responded, in his coarse, offhand way, "Fire the fucking thing!" the gunner shut his eyes and pulled the trigger and the gleaming Lewis exploded in a fusillade of shots, flying out over the Pacific in the general direction of Japan. It was only a second or two before the gun jammed and its crew, with cries of "Second position stoppage!" flung themselves upon it and began to disassemble its oily components, but it was long enough to convince us all that we carried with us a powerful punch, and even the cook, removing his hands from his ears and making his way back to his galley, was heard to agree that it had been a good show.

The make-believe aspect of our constant patrolling, of course, was that if we encountered anything — and in the years before Japan entered the war, what would we encounter on the West Coast? — we were totally unable to do much about it. Things were different in the East, where patrol vessels at least carried a few depth-charges and a gun of some sort, but even there in the early years nobody ever found any enemy lurking in the innumerable deserted bays of the Canadian coastline, nor did they really expect to. But it had to be done, if only as a matter of form, in the same way a policeman checks shop-door locks while walking his beat. And, of course, somebody had to examine all vessels entering a defended port, as we tried to assure ourselves as we rolled, for days on end, off Sambro light or William Head, or Point Grey. Bad weather was the real enemy that Canada's patrol and examination vessels had to face, and they bore with it for six long years.

There was that frightful battering given the *Cougar*, for instance. *Cougar*, formerly the luxury yacht *Breezin' Thru*, was a pretty little twin-screw diesel vessel whose raised fo'c'sle, low profile, two fat funnels, and rakish air gave her the appearance of a miniature destroyer, while an ancient Hotchkiss six-pound popgun, once mounted in the "fighting top" of some Victorian battlewagon and now standing proudly in front of her tiny bridge, imparted a distinctly warlike air. All during our gunnery training period in Naden barracks, we had lusted after her as she lay fitting out in the old Esquimalt dry dock, and hoped we might be lucky enough to be posted to her when we were sent off to sea. Alas! The posting went to Bill Gilmore, a beefy ex-lacrosse-player classmate of ours who cared nothing for her elegant lines and would have preferred something more like the robust tow-boats to which he was accustomed. And a month or two later we were to see his point when *Cougar* berthed near us after taking a proper dusting off Cape Flattery. Bill, his eyes puffy and red from lack of sleep, showed us around his stricken little ship, which had been shipping seas green over her short fo'c'sle. The wheel-house and asdic-cabin windows had been smashed in, and amidships she had been virtually submerged, her decks distorted, ventilators torn away, skylights smashed. Salt water had saturated her electrical circuits, starting a series of fires, and she had been forced to operate without lights. Crew spaces and galley were flooded out, and the pumps were still working on clearing the more than four feet of water from her bilges.

After that, we learned to look for more than sleek good looks in any ship intended to keep the sea in all weather.

Aboard our own little yacht, our adventures were less strenuous. Patrols through the remote Queen Charlotte Islands were full of wonders; we motored in awed silence up mirror-like fjords overhung by snow-capped mountains, watching enormous flocks of geese circling above us while mountain sheep stared from nearby slopes. Wildlife was unbelievably abundant. Coming into an anchorage one night and using our searchlight to pick up the beach, we found ourselves encircled by dozens of pairs of green eyes reflecting back the light from the woods about us. We speculated afterward on what they could be. Deer? Cougars? Bear? Our engineer, a cynical type, dismissed the lot as rabbits or rodents, but we held out for something bigger; grizzlies, maybe.

But such patrols were all too infrequent; mostly our days were spent swinging around a buoy in the rain off Metlakatla

Pass or Barrett Rock, the two approaches to Prince Rupert. Yet even there we had much to learn; we learned about handling ships in the constant berthing and manoeuvring which is the lot of an examination vessel, and we learned about handling men in looking after our little ship's company, a dozen diverse characters of widely varying backgrounds. We did it the hard way in small ships, without the help of big-ship routines and personnel; we learned to strike a balance between the discipline necessary to run an efficient ship and the easy tolerance essential to the close quarters of our tiny vessel. There were awkward moments. Facing down a fighting-drunk seaman without physical contact, for example, could be a character-building exercise, but there were many compensations. Yarning with examination officer Woody Thomson in the long, black hours of the middle watch was one of them; Woody was a graduate of Cambridge, and we could forget the West Coast rain in his tales of college dons and "bulldogs" in that lovely old place on the soft green banks of the faraway Cam. From signalman George Burrell, himself soon to be commissioned as an officer, we heard a lot about Calgary, a town we'd never visited. We learned to send and receive messages by Aldis light at something like professional speed, and to this day we can spell out the dots and dashes of the usual challenge to an incoming vessel just about as fast as we can say, "What ship?"

Not much to show for all those long, rainy nights, but it's something.

Mind you, the examination service had other compensations. It could be exciting coming alongside some huge merchantman at night in bad weather, eyeing the narrow expanse of driven spray and water, brightly floodlit, between us and the shipside towering far above us, trying to gauge the moment to jump for the ladder.

It was particularly interesting to board one of the big Japanese passenger liners of the NYK line, in those pre-Pearl Harbor days, and to come out of the wild rain and tumult into the sudden warmth and opulence of a sort of seagoing hotel lobby, and be led by politely hissing attendants up grand staircases and down carpeted corridors and past walls of mirrors and potted palms to the luxurious quarters of the captain of the *Something-or-other Maru*.

But the highlight of the examination service off Victoria was undoubtedly the debut of a new examination officer, a former classmate of ours and an exceptionally vigorous and determined young fellow. For some reason, nobody had explained to him that the CPR steamers on their daily service runs from Vancouver were allowed entrance into harbour without examination, merely flying the appropriate code flags which identified them.

As the afternoon steamer from Vancouver approached — let us call her the *Princess Thelma* — a fine sight with a bone in her teeth as she cracked along at full speed, the little grey-painted examination vessel closed her, signalling her furiously to stop. Without so much as a wave, the *Princess Thelma* surged past, leaving my friend the examination officer livid with indignation. Without a second's hesitation he called up the shore battery and ordered it to fire a shot across the bows of the errant *Princess*.

The duty gun's crew ashore, picking their teeth in the somnolent sunshine, could scarcely believe their good fortune; never before had they been called upon to actually fire a shot in, as you might say, anger. Leaping to their task with gleeful haste, they sent a shell whistling past the *Thelma*'s bows, raising an almighty splash in the blue sea half a mile beyond, and then, when the ship took no action, the gunners fired a further shot which sent a waterspout towering up a scant hundred yards from the *Thelma*'s bows.

The result was dramatic. Bells jangled on the *Princess Thelma*'s bridge, the sea frothed and boiled under her counter as her engines were put astern, and scores of white-faced passengers, alarmed by the sound of gunfire and the shuddering of the ship, lined the rails. Clouds of smoke and steam escaping from her funnels, the *Princess Thelma* at last lay motionless, her anxious captain, megaphone in hand, leaning over her bridge rail as the little examination vessel ranged close alongside. Had the port been closed because of plague or pestilence? Was there an enemy minefield ahead? He listened anxiously while the examination officer spoke into his loud hailer.

"What ship is that?"

Since the *Princess Thelma*'s name was painted above the questioner's head in letters four feet high, and she was as regular a feature of the Victoria day as the sun rising in the east, her incredulous captain was temporarily bereft of speech. Once recovered, however, he directed a stream of invective against the examination officer standing impassively below; he fairly danced with fury as the enormity of the thing came home to him. He called his tormentor nine kinds of an idiot, damned him for an impertinent incompetent, and consigned him, and his heirs and descendants, to everlasting hell-fire as he resumed course for harbour.

Signal, from Examination Officer to Shore Battery: "SHIP IS FRIENDLY."

Things were easier in West Coast ports south of the border, as the aircraft carrier HMS *Shah*, fresh from the builder's yard at Vancouver, discovered when entering San Francisco on her maiden voyage.

From port war signal station: "WHAT SHIP?"

From *Shah*: "HMSSHAH."

Port war signal station: "REPEAT."

After several repeats: "NEVER MIND WE WILL FIND OUT WHEN YOU GET IN."

Right from the beginning there was something faintly comic about naval proceedings on the West Coast, something about the atmosphere that rendered the most warlike proceedings a joke. The soft sunshine, the softer rain clouds misting sea and mountain, the colloquial Indian references to the "chuck" (sea) and "klooch" (woman) — the whole thing was a world removed from the harsh realities of European power politics and the Atlantic battle. Even after the Japanese bombed Pearl Harbor, the Pacific war assumed an absurd aspect when it finally reached the West Coast. A submarine, the only enemy sighted from our Pacific shores, lobbed shells ineffectually at a remote lighthouse on Estevan Point, on darkest Vancouver Island, while her compatriots launched incendiary balloons, made of bamboo and tissue paper, from far at sea in the hope of setting the Canadian rain forest alight; the whole West Coast war was pure opéra bouffe.

For those of us who did our training there, the West Coast offered a sort of innocent childhood before encountering the stresses and hardships that awaited us in the grown-up world, the real world of the North Atlantic. We had a great deal to learn about the navy, the sea, the war, and, for those of us too young to qualify for a commission as lieutenant, about Life, which was generally assumed to involve that most intriguing mystery of them all, Woman.

At a barracks bull-session it was a little dismaying to discover that we could produce only one sub-lieutenant out of the entire wardroom of HMCS *Naden*, the Esquimalt naval establishment — a spotty specimen from Prince Rupert — who had actually "had" a woman, a claim that won him instant respect and imparted enormous weight to his every pronouncement upon the opposite sex.

For the rest of us, the subject was to remain largely a closed book, despite our best efforts. Even fashion, it was conceded, was not conducive to gallantry; it was the age of the girdle, fitted with panels of Lastex capable of frustrating the most assiduous groper.

A fellow had to be both patient and persuasive to get a girl into trouble on the West Coast.

Part of the problem was opportunity, or rather the lack of it. For although Woodward's department store was full of dazzling girls, Victoria in the early months of the Second World War hardly rated as the Paris of the Pacific. For those of us hell-bent on living life to the full in the fast lane, Billy Tickle and his orchestra played for the Saturday-night supper dance in the ballroom of the Empress Hotel, as traditional a part of that venerable institution as its tea hour or its rose garden. You had to make the most of every waltz and decorous foxtrot, too, for at the very stroke of midnight Billy and his boys rose to their feet, squeaked out a tinny version of "The King", and then sloped off out the back way, switching off the bandstand lights as they went.

This was the signal for the clattering entry of an army of waiters, who stacked all the vacant chairs upside down on the tables before making a noisy exit. By this time the most determined merrymaker began to grasp that the revels were at an end, and the party gradually melted away. Beyond the ballroom door, the staid old hotel had blown down boilers and settled in for the night; we made our way, two by two, through the shadowy lobby under the censorious eye of the night clerk and stole out into the darkness beyond.

Still, what with the shortage of cars on the coast and the price of taxis, chances were you might get to walk your girl home, and with any luck you could take the long way round through Beacon Hill Park. And if the sun shone next morning, you could always find a friend and a couple of girls willing to rent wheels from the Shady Pergola Bicycle Rentery and pedal off to a picnic at Elk Lake, or a weenie roast among the driftwood logs on some secluded beach.

The liveliest of all West Coast functions were the ships' dances given by the companies of the new corvettes fitting out at Esquimalt, and generally held at the Crystal Gardens, a big ballroom that was part of the public swimming-pool complex behind the Empress in downtown Victoria. These were always good fun, with either a live orchestra or "big band" records on the juke box, and between dances you could promenade about and savour the smell of the chlorine wafting up from the pools below.

That was about as depraved as we were allowed to get, being debarred because of our exalted rank — sub-lieutenant, probationary, temporary — from drinking beer with the lower orders in the End House, the Coach and Horses, and other similar establishments where our sailors could enjoy themselves; moreover, as measly single-stripers — wavy navy at that — we had to tread lightly in the *Naden* wardroom, where we were allowed to mingle with our elders, and presumed betters, on sufferance only.

What with one thing and another, it was hard for a fellow to learn much about Life and Fast Women and all that sort of thing in Victoria, war or no war.

We did learn a bit, however, of our new trade. We learned about asdic, the supersonic detection of submerged submarines, aboard the *Sans Peur*, formerly the magnificent yacht of the Duke of Sutherland. We learned our gunnery ashore and did a night shoot aboard the auxiliary cruiser *Prince Robert*, formerly a Canadian National passenger liner. The first salvo from the *Robert*'s ancient six-inch guns scored a straddle on the towing tug, rather than on the target, and gave its crew their most exciting and memorable moments of the war.

On route marches we learned to swagger when marching "at attention" through crowded streets, and we experienced the thrill of being part of a disciplined body, a unit with its own pride and purpose. We were the King's Men, our sailors' legs moving as one to the steady, majestic naval pace, with hip scabbards swinging, tape ribbons flying, our fixed bayonets a flowing river of polished steel. An atavistic, almost primordial emotion, of course, much deplored in a later, effete age, and one we would not have missed for anything.

We learned that virtually everything in the gunnery world was done in line, usually by numbers; a snarled "Git fell in!" from some gunner's mate was the essential preliminary to every new experience, most of which would turn out to be unpleasant.

We learned ship-handling the hard way, by finding out what not to do when bringing the tugs and auxiliary vessels we practised on alongside. We learned, for example, not to take out the patrol vessel HMCS *Wolf* stern first. *Wolf*, a former luxury steam yacht with an exaggerated clipper bow, overhung the wharf so much when her stern was sprung out that her twenty-foot bowsprit reached across and wiped out several hundred dollars' worth of windows in the warehouse across the way, to the dismay of her skipper and the huge delight of our group of novitiates.

But, most of all, we learned about the navy; about its pride, its traditions, its mystique, the hierarchy and pecking order that made it work. We, in this war, were founding the traditions of our own navy, a new navy, but they were rooted in the foundations of "the Andrew", Britain's Royal Navy.

From this, the mother of all navies, we borrowed much of the pageantry that gives expression to the navy's *esprit de corps*. Sceptical though we were of pomp and circumstance, we could not help being moved by the almost sublime beauty of the navy's Sunset Ceremony, by the bugles calling, far and clear, above the measured music of the band as the white ensign, the embodiment of four centuries of sea power and of heaven-only-knows-how-many hard-fought victories, sank slowly down its staff with the setting of the sun.

But if naval ceremony could lift the heart, it could also terrify in its anger. It was at *Naden* that we saw our first "warrant" read, an experience not to be quickly forgotten. The whole of the ship's company was turned out and formed in hollow square to witness punishment. In the sudden silence after we had been drawn to attention, we could hear the prisoner and his escort being marched onto the "quarterdeck", their boots ringing on the pavement. The prisoner, ashen-faced and staring straight to his front, was paraded into the centre of the square between two burly "crushers", grim and smart in belt and gaiters, to the loud commands of the master-at-arms behind them, and halted with a crash of boots in front of the dais where *Naden*'s captain stood, in all the majesty of rank and office. The prisoner's cap was removed by one of his escorts and in a loud, clear voice the captain read the warrant, which set out the offences proved against the prisoner and the punishments to be assessed.

The wretched man had committed a long list of misdemeanours, but his most damning crime was desertion; from a fighting service in time of war, just about the ultimate offence.

But it was the reading of the punishments that was the most daunting part. For as each was proclaimed, an escort took from the prisoner some cherished mark or badge and threw it on the ground before him. He was to lose his good-conduct badge — "r-r-ripp!" — his substantive rank — "r-r-ripp" — and rating — "r-r-ripp!". With a few brief sentences the prisoner, who had marched in as one of us, a recognized member of our service family with all the familiar marks and badges attesting to his position in the service hierarchy, was reduced to a trembling wretch bereft of all the pride of uniform, a shambling nonentity cast out from the society of his fellows. With trembling lip and unseeing eyes, his ribbonless cap askew, he was led out of our sight to serve his time in some penal cell before a dishonourable discharge. He who had disgraced us had been himself disgraced. The navy had turned its back on him, a renunciation more terrible and absolute than any priestly excommunication, and one that left a moved and shaken ship's company behind.

It was all a little reminiscent of the regimental execution of a murderer in Kipling's "Danny Deever":

> For they've done with Danny Deever, you can hear the
> quickstep play,
> The regiment's in column and they're marching us away.
> Ho! The young recruits are shaking, and they'll want their
> beer today,
> After hanging Danny Deever in the morning.

Through all the long, lovely summer of 1940 our West Coast idyll continued, training ashore and afloat, and throughout the fall and winter we patrolled the hidden fjords of the northern coast, and the lost and lovely beaches of the Queen Charlottes. But in the early months of the new year, the first groundswell of events far off in the Atlantic began to reach our sheltered western shore. The first of the West Coast corvettes, building for months now at the yards of Wallace and Burrard, North Van and Yarrows, were nearing completion and we were avid to join them and be off to the great adventure that awaited them. The complement of each included one sub-lieutenant — any more, it was felt, would be too great a burden for so small a ship to shoulder — and by March nearly all of us had been posted to a corvette and were caught up in the frantic round of tests and trials, of manning and storing and making ready, that marks the commissioning of any warship, great or small.

They sailed us from Esquimalt, when we were ready, in pairs for mutual support on the long trip around through the Panama Canal. The little grey ships slipped away from the pretty, peaceful harbour, sounding their sirens in farewell to the groups of friends huddled on the headland to wave goodbye, before melting into the soft Pacific mists. They bore names from the province that had given them birth: *Kamloops* and *Agassiz*, *Trail* and *Nanaimo*, *Chilliwack* and *Alberni*, names that would become famous in the escort ports of the Atlantic.

Two by two when our time came we took our departure from this lovely land, leaving behind a stage in life as well as a place and people. We had come of age, and must put aside childish things. We said our goodbyes like men, promised to write, kissed our girls, and sailed away to the war on the other side of the world.

We could never come back.

Even on the Atlantic shore, once one got away from the more warlike hurly-burly of Halifax and Sydney, things were pretty peaceful in the early years of the war. There were ships being built in Saint John and refitted in a dozen little ports like Liverpool, Lunenburg, Pictou, Dalhousie, and so on, but all up the eastern seaboard, from Yarmouth and the southern tip of Nova Scotia northward to Gaspé and westward up the enormous estuary of the St. Lawrence to Quebec City, a thousand miles away, Canadian coastal towns snoozed peacefully, going about their normal business untroubled by the terrible events taking place somewhere beyond the eastern horizon.

Nowhere was this sense of sheltered calm more felt than in the placid river ports of old Quebec, the little French-speaking towns that had been there since before there was a Canada. Isolated from the rest of the country by language and culture, the people of the St. Lawrence pursued their age-old tasks of fishing the river and tilling the land quite oblivious of the outside world, and of the war which was the affair of the "*maudits anglais*".

Into this serene and sunlit world, on a bright spring morning in May 1942, swam a German U-boat. She was *U-553*, commanded by Lieutenant-Commander Thurmann, and she was about to change the serene world of the St. Lawrence forever.

THE GULF WAR

THE RIVER RUN

THURMANN was a thoroughly frustrated man after a voyage that had been a succession of failures and disappointments. Setting out from St. Nazaire for America, he had failed in stalks of a solitary merchantman and a passing frigate. Arriving off Boston, looking forward to good hunting there, he had been chagrined to find the cupboard bare of everything save escorted convoys bound for Halifax. Heading north and poking disconsolately about the Newfoundland coast, he had allowed himself to be spotted by the lighthouse-keeper at Cape Ray and had been subjected to aircraft attacks as a consequence, which had badly ruffled his nerves. It was a mean and hungry U-boat that prowled around the south shore of Anticosti Island and upriver, to finally lie in wait, in the gathering darkness, off Cap des Rosiers, on the river's south bank.

He had not long to wait. A British freighter, the SS *Nicoya*, hove into sight outward bound near midnight, and at point-blank range Thurman put two torpedoes into her. *Nicoya* began to sink immediately, her hull gaping in two enormous holes, and *U-553* drew off to the northeast, only to encounter the Dutch freighter *Leto*. Thurmann fired a torpedo into her, also at very close range, and then disengaged to the eastward, to lie on the bottom at the river entrance and savour his sinkings, the first for his U-boat, and, as it transpired, also the last; plagued by engine problems, *U-553* was forced to trundle home.

Thurmann could, of course, have no conception of the stir he had caused; two small merchantmen were an insignificant bag for a submarine in the context of the world struggle. But the explosion of his torpedoes had been heard and seen by hundreds of Quebec villagers ashore, and the appearance shortly thereafter of dozens of exhausted, oil-soaked survivors, together with dead and injured shipmates, had stunned the peaceful little riverside communities. Crowds gathered to view the scene, to sniff at the oil slicks covering the shoreline, to trade stories of death and disaster, and to peer fearfully out at the placid river and speculate on what might still be out there. The war — that "Englishman's war" occasionally reported in their newspapers — had suddenly and violently intruded into their placid French-Canadian world, and immediately the cry went up for the government — any government — to do something about it.

Almost as bad as the sinkings themselves, in the eyes of affronted Quebec villagers, was the censored official version of the torpedoings. The government merely announced that "a ship" had been lost, somewhere off the east coast; not a mention of the other ship sunk, or of the location of the sinkings, right in their river and not off some remote and alien east coast. Censorship was intended to keep details from being learned by the enemy, details that could tell expert intelligence officers much, and could, if they indicated ease of attack and richness of rewards, encourage further enemy action in a vulnerable area.

And the truth was that the St. Lawrence gulf, the whole vast area in the lee of Newfoundland to the east and the yawning Quebec shoreline on the other three sides, was especially vulnerable to submarine attacks owing to the unique characteristics of the water that filled it. Enormous quantities of cold fresh water, the accumulated runoff of half a continent, poured from the river into the relatively warm salt water of the Atlantic. The gulf was a huge mixing-ground of fresh and salt, cold and warm, and the subsequent layering of the water into strata, each level at a slightly different temperature from those above and below it, made the sonar sets of the day almost totally useless. The supersonic transmissions of the sonar were reflected back from the thermal layers, giving a multiplicity of vaguely defined echoes and making the detection of any submarine in the layered water virtually impossible.

If an escort ship could catch a U-boat on the surface, or just submerging, it might have a hope of destroying it; otherwise a submerged submarine was safe as a church anywhere in the Gulf. Allied naval command knew of this terrible vulnerability, and they were determined to do everything possible to keep the enemy from recognizing it.

The official close-mouthed policy quickly enraged not only the St. Lawrence villagers, anxious that something be done about the enemy ravening at their doorstep, but also their counterparts throughout the province, suddenly jolted into angry recognition that a hitherto alien conflict was impinging on their shores. The member of Parliament for Gaspé, Sasseville Roy, filled the House of Commons with demands for government action to halt what he implied might be an incipient Nazi invasion. What were Canadian ships and men doing messing about in distant theatres of war when they should be at home defending their loved ones?

An elected government in Ottawa, heavily dependent upon its solid support in Quebec, could not ignore the outcry of alarm from that province, even though its service chiefs dismissed any local fantasies of invasion, or even of any serious harm or injury being done to people on shore by U-boats in the river. Politics is the art of compromise, and the government now compromised between the demands of its electorate and the advice of its service commanders. A small naval force was withdrawn from the Atlantic to serve in the St. Lawrence; it was large enough to hinder Allied effort in the Atlantic battle, now reaching its decisive stages, yet too small to effectively close the river to U-boats.

It was a classic example of democracy at work: the government had been seen to respond to popular demand, and the results of that response, however damaging, were clearly no longer a part of any government responsibility.

Traffic on the river, never heavy once the convoy system had focussed shipping at Sydney and Halifax, had been suspended following the initial sinkings in the river, but the Gulf now became a centre of intense activity in other ways. The sleepy little village of Gaspé, at the southeast corner of the Gulf, was converted overnight into a naval base, HMCS *Fort Ramsay*, complete with boom defence, barracks, and a shore staff sufficient to spread alarm and confusion abroad, and excitement and enthusiasm among the village girls. In the picturesque little port in the shadow of Percé Rock was assembled a curious collection of warships which were to supply escorts for the tiny convoys in which river traffic would henceforth travel: a handful of corvettes and Bangors, an armed yacht, and a couple of flotillas of Fairmile motor launches.

These last represented yet another government compromise, made at the outbreak of war when the need for coastal patrol and escort craft became urgent. Short of the money and the time needed to furnish larger vessels, the government had settled for a flock of wooden-hulled, 112-foot, twin-engined, gasoline-powered motor boats. Staunch and sturdy, with diagonally planked hulls, they were excellent in the English Channel chop for which the British Fairmile firm had designed them, but they could be terrifying in the heavy Atlantic weather and fierce Canadian winters in which they were operated by the RCN. For these craft, the river was a welcome haven from the rockbound coasts of Newfoundland and the Maritimes, and they settled into their new base happily enough.

Their operational effectiveness against U-boats was, to put it charitably, questionable. Commanded and crewed by some of the keenest young fellows in the service, their brisk and warlike appearance was somewhat deceiving. Since they were relatively slow, their big tanks of volatile gasoline made them terribly vulnerable to enemy fire of the lightest calibre, while their own armament — a few depth-charges, tiny guns, primitive sonar and radar — was hardly overwhelming. They operated on the mosquito principle: negligible individually, they could be a nuisance in a swarm, and to watch them weaving slowly nose to tail, ringed about a suspected underwater contact, was like being spectator to some age-old religious rite, filled with mystery and a sense of impending doom.

Into this little world of tiny bases, tiny convoys, tiny ships and escorts, all set within the cosy confines of a green and pleasant river, we corvette types arrived like so many Gullivers in the land of Lilliput. Initially we were filled with resentment, being plucked away from our Newfoundland escort groups at the time of their cruellest testing, a time when the force had already been hard hit by the detaching of ten corvettes to screen the new Aruba-Halifax oil convoys of fast tankers. For corvette crews accustomed to the great Atlantic convoys, the handful of grubby lake freighters and ancient coastal coal-burners that constituted a river convoy hardly seemed worthy of the term, while the one, two, or three escorts assigned to each never added up to an effective screen. A lot of play-acting in a make-believe war, we assured ourselves, watching the convolutions of the Fairmiles frisking about our flanks with amused indulgence.

From Fairmile to next ahead, who has forgotten to recover fog buoy streamed astern, after fog has lifted: "TELL THE CAPTAIN THERE'S NO BEER LEFT IN THIS KEG."

It did not take long for our change of status to sink in. Out in the Atlantic, corvettes were small fry, the work-horses of the escort groups. But here in the river we were virtually major war vessels, the top of the power pyramid, bigger even than our old friends the Bangors, and we revelled in a new sense of our importance. This river war might turn out to be not such a bad business after all, we told ourselves as we steamed up the placid St. Lawrence, taking advantage of the summer sunshine to paint around our upper deck, everyone stripped to the waist to begin his Quebec tan.

We arrived at Quebec City as trim and smart as any peace-time yacht, and berthed in the St. Charles basin there alongside the corvette *Shawinigan*, with whose affable ship's company we soon struck up a close and easy friendship.

The city we had arrived at, and in which we were to be based for some memorable months, was like nothing we had experienced before. To us English-speaking Canadians — "*Anglos*" — its language and culture were utterly alien, and its remoteness from the war, and from the restrictions and austerities of wartime Canada, gave it the ambience of some small European city, some little capital low down in the Balkans, say.

It had a surprisingly gay and sophisticated night life, based on the great dining-rooms of the Château Frontenac and a handful of elegant restaurants; the food and drink were exceptional, and the theatres and orchestras were lively if limited. But, above all, it was a walled town, with its citadel and the turrets of the Château Frontenac, a baronial castle masquerading as a hotel, towering on the cliffs high above the river. Filled with parks, churches, and public buildings, it was the most picturesque city we had yet encountered, and in no time at all it had clasped us to its Gallic bosom.

Indeed, for some that was more than a figure of speech; the city fairly teemed with pretty girls, bright of eye and wit and with all the chic flair and elegance popularly attributed to French girls. Quebec City was Canada's Paris in the spring, and to stroll hand in hand with some ravishing girl along a boulevard, or through parks bright with spring greenery, was pretty intoxicating stuff for fellows whose last date had been with someone in a head-scarf and galoshes in a grubby Glace Bay café. In no time at all, it seemed just about everyone had made himself at home in Quebec, and weekends in port were filled with picnics at Montmorency Falls, lunches on Dufferin Terrace overlooking the river, and dancing at the Château or on the special ballroom cruises run by the Lévis ferries, their tiers of lights bright across the dark water. Within a month, our fellows were beginning to feature in local engagement notices, and before the summer was out whole ships' companies were being invited to wedding receptions, almost as a matter of course.

Not that everything was sweetness and light. A lot of young fellows in town resented this naval intrusion into their preserve, and a good many local people muttered imprecations under their breath when we got onto a streetcar or into a theatre line-up with them. You could get beaten up in an alley if you weren't careful, and if you had had a drink too many, you could expect no mercy from the local police, who would work you over at the station before tossing you into a cell.

On one memorable evening, two corvette officers, dining alone at the Château supper-dance, invited the chanteuse to join them at their ringside table after she had finished her number. She sat down cheerfully enough, but some noisy young fellows at a nearby table took umbrage. Things got a bit physical; all unknowing, the locals were in over their heads, for one of our corvette types was a burly ex-policeman from Winnipeg. He picked the young lady up and planted her on the bandstand, out of harm's way, before settling down to fixing the wagon of his first pair of assailants. These two, it now appeared, had friends near at hand, friends who seemed to thirst for Winnipeg blood.

But these Prairie policemen are tough hombres. With the experience born of a hundred such punch-ups, our man quickly made a tactical withdrawal up onto the bandstand, dragging his friend, a young subbie who had just joined the ship, along with him, to make a stand, back to back, in the midst of the orchestra. By the time the two had sorted out all comers, there were bits of bandsmen and instruments in various stages of disrepair all over the place; it became a sort of epic stand, stalwart English versus furious French, reminiscent of Harold's thanes at the Battle of Hastings.

Came a lull in the battle; our policeman's trained senses told him it was time for a swift strategic withdrawal. Before the shattered forces of the enemy could renew the assault, the two sailors were through the backstage door, down the stairs, and out into the cool night, the ex-policeman still clutching a dented cornet he had wrested from an irate trumpet-player. This, the spoils of victory, he bore from the battlefield, and the two returned, battered but triumphant, to the haven of their wardroom.

Fresh from the cloistered calm of the officers' training course at King's College, the young sub-lieutenant was now convinced that he had, indeed, joined a fighting service.

For most of us, however, who'd been invited into the warm, friendly circle of some French-Canadian household, Quebec was a most hospitable place, and over at HMCS *Montcalm*, the big naval reserve division, executive officer René St. Laurent, son of the distinguished politician, made all corvette officers feel at home.

Traffic along the river was reopened on our arrival, and two convoy systems were begun. Everything destined for overseas was sailed in convoy to Sydney, but our ship, the corvette *Trail*, accompanied initially by *Shawinigan*, was bound northward with convoys up the Labrador coast to Goose Bay. Here Canada was building an enormous air base, to be used, along with its Yankee counterpart at Thule in Greenland, for staging the fleets of bomber aircraft that were being ferried to Britain. *U-553*'s interruption was supposed to have delayed completion of the Goose Bay field by six months, so everyone was in a hurry to get things moving again, and for the next few months we had little enough time to savour the delights of old Quebec.

We alternated weary days of trundling along with a couple of coal-burning clunkers — the *Carolus* and the *Fleurus* — eked out by an occasional old coaster or lake steamer, with the high-speed passages of the *Lady Rodney*, the former West Indian cruise ship. Loaded with construction workers and duty-free booze, this old girl virtually flew down the river and up the coast, leaving us to hang on as best we could. Lord Haw-Haw, in his regular Berlin broadcasts, had promised that the *Lady Rodney* would be sunk within a month, and her skipper was in no mood to ease down merely to accommodate a lousy sixteen-knot corvette; we ran flat out and hoped that the Chief and his boiler-room brigade would be able to cope.

It was a strange run, like nothing we had ever experienced before; often we were in sight of land, and the scenery up the Labrador coast was magnificent. Low hills, heavily wooded, alternated with stark mountains and cliffs of naked rock rising abruptly from the sea. Often there was so much iron that the very rock wept with rust, and our magnetic compass spun uselessly in circles, while the occasional uncharted rock or reef emphasized the sketchiness of the existing coastal surveys. The few settlements were tiny affairs: a clutch of sheds and shacks behind a spindly wharf, usually centred on the inevitable white-painted fur-trading post. Rigolet, at the mouth of Hamilton Inlet, was such a place; we landed an officer and a couple of signalmen there to establish a naval control post. When we picked them up at the end of the shipping season months later, the elegant officer and the fresh-faced young signalmen had quite disappeared, leaving a trio of brown and bearded fellows rigged out in sealskin mukluks and fox-fur jackets, and full of outlandish stories.

Lake Melville, at the top of Hamilton Inlet, was the end of the line for us; here we anchored while our convoy off-loaded its cargo. The airfield construction workers were earning fabulous wages, and were desperate to spend it; *Lady Rodney*'s crewmen did a brisk, and illicit, trade in liquor, flogging three-dollar bottles for thirty dollars on a seller's market.

Goose Bay was a man-made intrusion into a wild and desolate world, where man clung by his fingertips to the very edge of a cold wasteland. Everywhere about us was virgin territory; only a few miles to the north the Germans took advantage of the remoteness of this coast to establish a permanent foothold. It was their only successful lodgement on the North American continent, and it was so secret that it remained undiscovered for more than thirty years.

To plan their military operations, it was essential for the German high command to have some foreknowledge of the weather conditions likely to prevail over Europe, and as their weather systems arrived from the western Atlantic it was in this area that they concentrated their efforts. U-boats included weather reports in their regular reports to base, and some released drifting "weather buoys", which, powered by batteries, automatically transmitted weather data in the area back to Germany.

But the life of such buoys was severely limited, and they were no substitute for a permanent weather-reporting station on the American continent. Accordingly, *U-537* was dispatched in the fall of 1942 to set up a permanent weather station, code-named "Kurt", on the northern coast of Labrador, sufficiently remote from any settlement to escape detection. Arrived off Cape Chidley, the northern tip of Labrador, Kapitänleutnant Peter Schrewe worked his U-boat slowly southward among the uncharted reefs and rocks until he rounded the southern tip of the Hutton Peninsula and anchored thankfully off the deserted shoreline of Martin Bay. On the afternoon of October 22 he landed a few seamen, who took up position on nearby hills as lookouts and sentries, while the technical experts he carried directed a working party in the setting up of the weather-reporting station. "Kurt" consisted of a set of meteorological instruments, a 150-watt short-wave transmitter, a ten-metre antenna, and an array of nickel-cadmium and dry-cell batteries. Working through the night in a light frost, the party had the job finished by the following afternoon, and at 1800 hours Schrewe and his men had the satisfaction of hearing the station transmit its first automatic weather report. It continued to do so, month after month, until its batteries eventually went flat, after which the little weather station remained, unnoticed and untouched, until its eventual discovery by Canadian authorities in July 1981. A chance remark by a former crewman of *U-537*, overheard by a British journalist, led RCMP officers to the scene and "Kurt", still in good shape, was packed up and shipped off to go on public display in Ottawa.

In 1942 the Labrador run brought its own problems: the occasional iceberg, or an icefield jamming the Strait of Belle Isle, and dense fog in the Gulf or the river, made even more scary by the little local motor schooners, staggering under mountainous deckloads of pulpwood, plying unconcernedly back and forth without lights or sound signals of any sort. The lake steamers, too, could be a nuisance; slab-sided and under-powered, they were never intended to stand up to ocean conditions, and even a moderate blow in the Gulf could make them unmanageable, unable to alter course to windward.

But by and large those early summer months of 1942 were an idyllic interlude for us, a welcome escape from the grim Atlantic battle, but a holiday that was already coming to a close.

On the night of July 6, a German U-boat, *U-132*, specially briefed by Dönitz himself, surfaced in the midst of a Sydney-bound convoy off the Gaspé peninsula and fired four torpedoes at the nearest ships, dark shadows in the night. One torpedo missed, and was later found stranded on the shore, but the other three struck home, and three little merchantmen — *Dinaric*, *Hainaut*, and *Anastasias* — sank in the relatively shallow waters of the Gulf.

However, *U-132* was illuminated by the star shell fired by an escort, the Bangor HMCS *Drummondville*, and when she dived to escape she was caught by the subsequent pattern of depth-charges and so badly mauled that she was forced to head for home, trailing long ribbons of oil behind her. But she still had a sting in her tail; en route she ran into a Sydney-Quebec convoy and put a torpedo into the SS *Frederika Lensen*, which, towed into a nearby anchorage by the corvette *Weyburn*, subsequently sank.

King of the Gulf

It was in late August that Paul Hartwig, the most celebrated of all the U-boat commanders operating on this side of the Atlantic and the man whose name was to become synonymous with the Battle of the St. Lawrence, swaggered onto the Canadian stage.

Lieutenant-Commander Paul Hartwig was the archetypal German submariner, a hard-drinking roisterer ashore and daring, shrewd, and tenacious afloat. Scion of a military family and brought up in the Prussian tradition, he had served in the pre-war regular navy and had survived a U-boat cruise in the war-time Atlantic before being given command of *U-517*.

His iron nerve and resolution, as well as his hard drinking, made him greatly admired by his fifty-man crew, and he arrived in the Gulf determined to sink the 80,000 tons of shipping required to qualify for his Knight Commander's Iron Cross, and thus rank with the select few "aces" of the German U-boat arm.

Arrived on his patrol ground, Hartwig took up station in the narrows of the Strait of Belle Isle, south of Cape Bauld, the northernmost tip of Newfoundland, and it was here, on the night of August 27, that he encountered a little convoy of U.S. ships bound for the airfield at Thule in Greenland, escorted by a U.S.

Coast Guard cutter. Hartwig had no difficulty in torpedoing the army transport *Chatham*, a passenger ship loaded with construction workers, and watched with fascinated horror the results of his first-ever kill. Oddly for a man of his character, Hartwig was deeply moved by the death-throes of the doomed transport, viewed through his periscope, and he lectured his crew over the intercom system as the *Chatham* sank, taking twenty-three men with her. As Germans, he said, they must serve Germany, but they must realize that their enemy was also honourbound to his own cause. U-boat men must remember that their turn to be sunk might be next, he cautioned; they must bear this in mind and accept any triumphs that came their way in a spirit of humility.

All in all, an odd and revealing homily from a Prussian determined to sink 80,000 tons of shipping for the sake of a decoration on his chest, but, as circumstances were to prove, Hartwig was a man of complex character. Elated by his success, he surfaced next morning and sent off a report to U-boat headquarters, a proceeding he was quickly to regret. His transmission was detected and accurately plotted by the wireless station at Harbour Grace, Newfoundland, and an RCAF aircraft, scrambled and sent to search down the bearing, nearly caught *U-517* napping, and she was forced to crash-dive to escape.

In the corvettes *Trail* and *Shawinigan*, we were escorting a convoy northbound for Goose Bay a hundred miles astern of the U.S. convoy attacked by Hartwig, and the next day we came upon *Chatham's* survivors. Most of them, jammed tightly into the ship's big lifeboats, were chilled and stiff after a night afloat in northern waters but were otherwise in good shape, but for those who had been forced to take to the water before managing to pull themselves out onto a life raft, the night had been a cruel ordeal. Many were covered in oil, the heavy bunker fuel that turns to a tar-like viscosity in cold water; others had been injured in trying to get clear of the ship, which had sunk in just three minutes. Some were dead, others would die, but we pulled them all over our low bulwarks, our fellows lining the waist and hanging in the scramble nets overside to help the survivors aboard and hustle them forward into the messdecks and the warm blankets that awaited them there.

Even as we tended the victims of the previous night's sinking, Hartwig was manoeuvring *U-517* into position to pluck yet another victim from the thinly escorted convoy he'd discovered. While doing so, he encountered another U-boat, *U-165*, on the surface, and arranged a joint attack before they were both forced to crash-dive to avoid a patrolling aircraft. Surfacing at nightfall, the U-boats attacked from opposite sides, and each scored a hit, *U-165* torpedoing the SS *Arlyn* and *U-517* the SS *Laramie*. Counter-attacks were light, and both U-boats escaped without difficulty. *Arlyn* sank rapidly, with some loss of life, but *Laramie* managed to limp safely into port, despite a gaping hole in her side.

After landing our dead at Battle Harbour and our survivors at Goose Bay, we were screening a homeward-bound convoy, running light, when we encountered Hartwig again. A foul-up by a staff officer had routed our southbound group so that we would pass a northbound convoy in the Strait of Belle Isle, the narrow confines of which restricted movement, making this the most dangerous and vulnerable part of the northern run, hemmed in as we were by high and menacing shorelines on each side. At the very moment of contact, when *Shawinigan*, on our port side, had just detected and identified the outermost escort of the oncoming convoy, Hartwig brought *U-517* in on

A sort of innocent childhood before the grown-up world of the North Atlantic — sub-lieutenants in training at HMCS *Naden*, in Esquimalt, B.C. Author at left.

A charade — the ship's company of His Majesty's Canadian Ship *Cancolim*, a yacht armed with a stripped Lewis gun. Author at left.

Pre-sailing convoy conference at Admiralty House, March 1941. Merchant-ship captains examine their convoy sailing orders while naval staff officers, at the fireplace, explain the details. (Public Archives Canada/PA-105297)

Ships assembling in Bedford Basin for a convoy to Britain. (Canadian Forces/REA-391-5)

Under the lee of a screening destroyer, column leaders of an eastbound convoy plough steadily toward a distant port. (Canadian Forces/A-133)

A rare aerial photo of a convoy at sea, each ship at the end of a long wake of churned-up water. (Courtesy of Graham McBride)

''Newfyjohn'': the wartime base for many North Atlantic escort groups was the busy harbour of St. John's, Newfoundland. Most commercial ships berthed at the finger piers of the city waterfront in the foreground, while warships lay along the jetties of the south side, opposite. (Public Archives Canada/PMR 84-731)

Helped by harbour tugs, the salvage vessel *Foundation Franklin* eases a torpedoed merchantman through the boom defence gate at the entrance to St. John's, Newfoundland, in the wintry setting familiar to thousands of wartime sailors. (Public Archives Canada/PMR 83-1372)

Like a packet of fags on a pencil — HMCS *St. Croix*, a typical four-stacker and one of the fifty destroyers handed over by the United States, the most dubious gift since the Greeks left that wooden horse for the Trojans.

A typical escort in the Gulf War: HMCS *Trail* in the new (1942) camouflage but still with a short fo'c'sle and her mast forward of her bridge, topped with the infamous SW1C radar "rake".

A seaman fights for his life as he attempts to clear the tons of ice threatening to capsize his corvette on a midwinter Triangle Run.

The Bangor minesweeper HMCS *Clayoquot* was torpedoed and lost off the Sambro light vessel on Christmas Eve, 1944, with the loss of eight of her crewmen. (Canadian Forces)

Soaked in fuel oil and shivering in the December cold, survivors from the torpedoed *Clayoquot* struggle for their lives. (Canadian Forces/GM-3001)

Each with its 271 radar "lighthouse" towering above its bridge, a group of corvettes, including HMCS *Dundas*, *Chilliwack*, and *Arrowhead*, lies alongside Halifax dockyard. (Courtesy of Thomas Lynch)

Fresh from the builder's yard, the new Canadian frigate HMCS *Valleyfield* picks her way through the drifting ice of a wintry St. Lawrence River on her way to the sea in December 1943. (RCN photograph/CN6504)

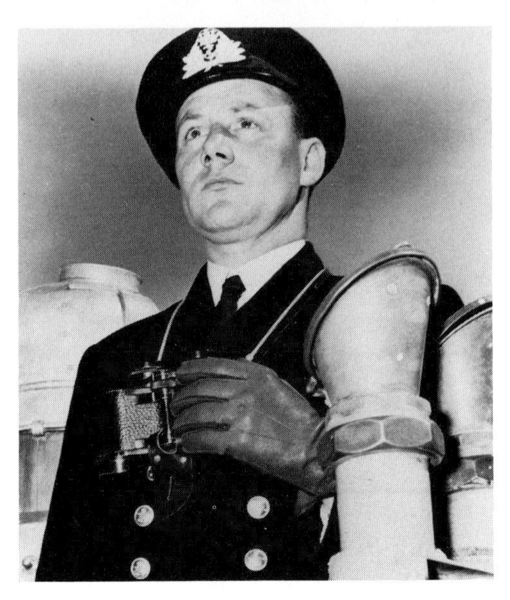

Lieutenant-Commander Charles Petersen, Royal Canadian Naval Reserve, commanding officer of the Canadian corvette HMCS *Giffard*, photographed on the bridge of his ship on her arrival in St. John's, Newfoundland, with the survivors of the frigate *Valleyfield*. (RCN photograph/Z-288)

Commodore Cuthbert Taylor, Royal Canadian Navy, Flag Officer, Newfoundland, stands to attention with cane tucked under his arm as the funeral party bearing the flag-draped coffin of *Valleyfield*'s Lieutenant Frank Reynolds, RCNVR, arrives at the hillside cemetery in St. John's, Newfoundland.

the surface to attack the northbound ships. The corvette *Weyburn* sighted the wash from the U-boat conning-tower and Tom Golby, her captain, immediately bore down on Hartwig at full speed, illuminating the U-boat with rockets and getting off a couple of rounds from his forward gun. But Hartwig was a cool customer; waiting till *Weyburn* was nearly on him, he fired a torpedo into the convoy before crash-diving. *Weyburn*'s throwers jammed in the emergency, and she got away only two depth-charges as she crossed the swirl of the diving submarine, and while Hartwig's men got a bad shaking, the U-boat was unscathed.

Hartwig's torpedo had hit the old lake steamer *Donald Stewart*, loaded with cement and a big deckload of high-octane aviation gasoline. She exploded like a bomb and burned like a torch, the flames lighting up the water for miles around as bright as day, with a roar that appalled all of us. *Weyburn* quickly lost contact with *U-517* in the seething water left by her attack, and after half an hour's vain searching, she left to pick up *Donald Stewart*'s survivors, who had been fortunate enough to get a boat away quickly before flaming gasoline covered the whole surface of the sea around the doomed ship. White-faced and horrified — we'd watched a trapped crewman calmly turn to face the flames before the inferno consumed him — we in *Trail* and *Shawinigan* shepherded our own little flock past the dreadful scene, while the other convoy swept by in the opposite direction. It was a humbling experience for all of us.

Hartwig, occasionally in company with *U-165*, now began a systematic patrol of the Gulf, crossing and recrossing from side to side while steadily moving upriver. He was encountering an alarmed and aroused enemy now. Canadian authorities had managed to detach a few more Bangors for duty in the river, and air patrols had been greatly increased. It was a patrolling aircraft that nearly put *U-517* out of business. Catching the U-boat napping on the surface, she swept down out of a cloudless sky and dropped a bomb that caught *U-517* fair and square, striking just forward of the conning-tower and piercing the upper-deck casing. By a miracle she survived. The bomb, probably because of a faulty fuse, failed to detonate, and after waiting submerged, hardly daring to breathe, until the aircraft had departed, Hartwig surfaced again to examine the damage.

The bomb was protruding from a jagged hole in the submarine's superstructure, but the vital watertight pressure hull beneath was undamaged. While the rest of the crew remained utterly motionless, lest a slight tremor affect the delicate work, Hartwig and his engineer officer, with the assistance of two seamen, gently levered the slumbering bomb over the side.

It had been a narrow squeak, but there was more to come. Hartwig had been shifting his patrol upriver, until in early September he was within 250 miles of Quebec City, and so close to the shore that he could identify individual people through his periscope as he scrutinized each village. On a Saturday night, after charging his batteries, Hartwig took the U-boat in to within yards of a town pier so that his men could enjoy the music wafting out over the water from the local dance-hall.

Early on the morning of September 6, Hartwig made contact with *U-165*, and by nightfall the two had set up a patrol line opposite Cap Chat, each U-boat trimmed down on the surface and close in to the shore, on opposite sides, so as to be invisible against the loom of the land. They had not long to wait.

Just before 10 p.m. a small convoy hove in sight, bound for Sydney and screened by the corvette *Arrowhead*, the Bangor *Truro*, the armed yacht *Raccoon*, and two Fairmile motor launches, *Q-64* and *Q-83*.

It was an interesting and unusual escort force, but the motley group was commanded by veteran and seasoned officers, including, in the Fairmiles, Bill Grand and Norm Williams, both volunteer-reserve officers with considerable river experience. They were led by the redoubtable Commander E. G. Skinner in *Arrowhead*, a celebrated character and a veteran of the Atlantic convoy runs, who had been a Newfoundland rum-runner before the war. At Gaspé earlier, Skinner had encountered the corvette *Charlottetown*. Her captain was Willard Bonner, one of the best of the RCNR officers, an outstanding commanding officer and a Cape Bretoner who, before the war, had commanded a patrol vessel in the marine division of the Royal Canadian Mounted Police and had frequently pursued illicit vessels commanded by Skinner. The reunion of these two, formerly pursuer and pursued, had been a memorable one, culminating in a tearful rendition of "Auld Lang Syne" and the pledging of eternal friendship. The *Raccoon* also was commanded by a Naval Reserve officer and a mutual friend of both Skinner and Bonner, Lieutenant J. N. Smith. She was more yacht than warship, but armed yacht crews could adapt to anything; one such yacht, HMCS *Renard*, bereft of charts, had once navigated herself from Pictou to Halifax with an Imperial Oil road map!

Plagued by the unreliable Canadian radar, and with sonar rendered almost useless by thermal layering in the river, Skinner had devised his own "shoot-from-the-hip" tactic. He emphasized to his group the need for immediate response to any enemy attack: head for the U-boat, fire at him with any gun that will bear, and when he submerges, drop full patterns of depth-charges over his diving point without even attempting to gain sonar contact. The usual refinements of U-boat hunting in the open Atlantic had no relevance here, where sonar contacts could be impossible and distances short. It was sound advice, and it was soon to be put into effect.

At about 10 p.m., *U-165*, turning towards the oncoming convoy, fired a torpedo which struck the little Greek steamer *Aeas*, the explosion blowing a large hole in the ship's side immediately under the bridge and killing the wireless operator and a fireman. The remainder of the crew took to their boats while *U-165*, unseen in the shadow of the hilly shoreline, quietly withdrew.

After a sonar search had failed to locate anything in the muddled conditions to be expected in the layered river water, the escorts rescued the Greek survivors from their boats and resumed station on the convoy, now some miles downriver.

The explosion caused by the torpedoing had rattled windows ashore, and the flash had been seen for miles, but after the convoy had passed on, a further couple of heavy explosions were noted, heard but not seen from within the convoy. Those two last "bumps in the night" were *Raccoon*'s requiem. As *U-165* was withdrawing astern, she had stumbled across the little armed yacht in her screening position out on the quarter of the convoy, and had pumped two torpedoes into her at close range. The "Coon" simply disappeared with all her complement of thirty-nine men. A few days later, some wreckage and the body of Lieutenant R. H. "Russ" McConnell, in happier days a notable McGill athlete, would wash ashore on Anticosti Island, the only trace of the yacht's sinking. For the rest, HMCS *Raccoon* and all her company had quietly vanished from the world, never to be seen again.

Hartwig now brought *U-517* in for the kill, closing in from his position on the bow of the convoy, but had the misfortune to encounter *Arrowhead* and a by now frustrated and angry Skinner. *U-517* promptly dived, but Skinner took *Arrowhead* over her diving position and, true to his shoot-from-the-hip formula, fired a full pattern of ten depth-charges over the site without waiting to establish firm sonar contact. It was a devastating attack, the worst ever experienced by Hartwig and his crew. *U-517*'s lights were blown out, leaving her in darkness relieved only by a handful of emergency lights; water spurted from fractured pipes in the engine room and men were knocked from their feet by the tremendous explosion of the depth-charges detonating all around them.

Hartwig was equal to the crisis, however; he quickly released a *Pillenwerfer*, a small perforated tin filled with a chemical that, on contact with water, released a cloud of bubbles that gave a solid target echo to any probing sonar, and behind this false echo, which baffled *Arrowhead*'s sonar operator, *U-517* quietly beat a retreat, bloodied but unbowed, her superficial damage quickly repaired.

Hartwig was determined to make the most of the tempting target posed by the slow river convoy, and as soon as *U-517* was restored to normal, he set off after his quarry.

He caught up with it with little trouble and, late on September 7, was lying submerged, waiting for darkness, when a group of three ships arrived from nearby Gaspé to join the downriver convoy. It was already dusk, and with typical daring Hartwig seized the unusual opportunity that the two groups of freighters afforded him. Surfacing between the two clusters of ships, he found targets in his sights both ahead and astern, and immediately fired both his bow tubes and his single stern tube at point-blank range. Every torpedo found its mark; almost simultaneously fountains of water erupted from the sides of three merchantmen, and Hartwig crash-dived, elated by his success; three hits in a single attack!

It had indeed been a notable feat, the greatest success scored by a U-boat in the Gulf and, as it turned out, the high point of Hartwig's career. All three ships hit sank quickly, the Greek *Mount Taygetos* carrying with her five men, all killed in the engine room where the torpedo struck. Her Greek sister ship, the *Mount Pindus*, also suffered the loss of an engineer and a fireman killed by the explosion, while the old lake steamer *Oakton*, hit in the engine room like the other pair, had an oiler and two firemen killed in the explosion, and her big St. Bernard dog, the ship's mascot, drowned when the freighter sank quickly. The Fairmile *Q-83* picked up no fewer than seventy-eight shivering, oil-soaked survivors and landed them later at Gaspé. Their legacy lingered on, however; *Q-83*'s seamen, who had cheerfully given up their blankets to their guests, were soon all itching and scratching. ''We eventually became expert in getting rid of crab lice,'' recalls Bill Grand, *Q-83*'s captain.

For all his success, Hartwig and *U-517* now became more hunted than hunter; time after time the U-boat was forced to dive to escape the attentions of the aerial patrols that now combed the waters between Anticosti Island and the Gaspé shore. Hartwig was determined to maintain his one-man war, however, until all his torpedoes had been expended, and he kept on station doggedly, recharging his batteries as best he could, an hour or two at a time, on the surface between shallow dives. His reward was to come three days after his great coup.

On the sombre, mist-clouded morning of September 11, HMCS *Charlottetown*, a relatively new corvette, and the Bangor HMCS *Clayoquot* were making their way downriver after delivering a convoy at Bic Island. They were steaming at twelve knots, their puny radar probing the thick clouds of swirling early-morning mist, their sonar virtually useless in the usual thermal-layering conditions. Hartwig heard them coming and quite by chance found himself in an ideal position to attack. Ever the opportunist, he got off two quick shots at close range, the torpedoes having a very short run before both crashed home on *Charlottetown*'s starboard quarter. The corvette immediately listed to starboard as water poured into her, and she began to sink rapidly.

Charlottetown's first lieutenant was George Moors, an old friend and Stone Frigate classmate of ours; a big, blue-eyed blond from Port Arthur with the broad shoulders and narrow waist of the oarsman and boxer he had been. An affable, easy-going manner cloaked a free and venturesome spirit; George would eventually find his niche as a motor-torpedo-boat commander in an English Channel flotilla. As *Charlottetown*'s executive officer he had come to admire and respect the knowledge and character of his captain, Willard Bonner; between the hard-bitten Cape Bretoner and his brash young subordinate was an almost filial affection.

Bonner, on the bridge when the torpedoes struck, immediately began to organize the getting away of the ship's boats, but as the ship listed ever more sharply to starboard, he quickly realized that the port boat was useless, and shifted all his attention to the starboard boat, which was cleared away and rapidly lowered to the water. As scores of sailors poured up from below decks, Bonner could see that time was precious as his ship sank ever lower, and he shouted: "Jump for it, boys; we're not going to make it." The forward Carley floats were both got away, and men now began to jump overside and swim, as best they could, for the relative safety of either boat or raft.

There were the usual incidents expected in moments of crisis;

one sailor went back below to fetch a photograph of his girl, left behind in his messdeck. He was never seen again. One man leaped overside clutching a bully-beef container; it floated, and held him up as well as any lifebuoy. Seaman Garland, who had helped pass out lifejackets, including his own, to shipmates who couldn't swim, was still clinging to the gun platform when the stricken corvette began to rear on end, her bows rising as her stern sank. As his shipmates in the boat urged him to jump, he shouted that he was going back to fetch the ship's mascot, Screech, a mongrel picked up in Newfoundland. He, too, was never seen again; the dog was already aboard a raft, and survived.

And now a terrible thing happened, the real tragedy of the sinking. *Charlottetown*, like all escorts, carried a pattern of depth-charges, set to explode at shallow depth, in her traps and throwers, ready for instant use. As the stern sank deep below the surface, the submerged charges went off in a shattering explosion of hundreds of pounds of high explosive, right in the midst of dozens of struggling swimmers. The fearful detonation of her own charges killed more of *Charlottetown*'s sailors than either of the two German torpedoes.

Hartwig, watching the scene through *U-517*'s periscope a safe distance away, was appalled at the carnage, even as his own submarine rocked to the blast of the distant explosion. He had little time to observe, however, as *Clayoquot* bore down on him, following what seemed to be a promising sonar echo. But at the last minute Lieutenant Lade, her captain, broke off the attack, because the water was filled with *Charlottetown* crewmen, living, dead, or injured. The possible success of any attack in those notoriously difficult sonar waters was outweighed by the certain death any depth-charge explosions would bring to so many swimmers. Nevertheless, *Clayoquot* persisted in the hunt for

U-517, as she was bound to do, hoping for a contact clear of the corvette survivors, while Hartwig tiptoed from the scene as his victim disappeared beneath the waters of the St. Lawrence.

In the corvette's boat, George Moors now began to organize the scattered survivors, pulling individual swimmers into the boat and directing the rafts to try and keep together, but increasingly his chief concern was his captain. What had happened to Bonner, the last man seen to leave the ship? In grim-faced silence, the survivors of *Charlottetown*'s shattered household set out to find their father, rowing slowly through the mists, now shredding with the growing day.

They found him at last, after a long search. He was floating upright in his lifejacket, but his distorted face showed how he had died, in the terrible detonation of the depth-charges. With a gentleness surprising in a big man, George lifted the slight body into the boat, where it was laid out with awkward reverence along the bottom boards by youngsters awed at the nearness of their dead captain. They set out again then, rowing as best they could for the distant shore, but it quickly became apparent that something would have to be done if the oarsmen were to find room to row in the overcrowded boat. Accordingly, George lifted Bonner's body back over the side, and others helped him secure the dead man's lifejacket to the rudder of the boat by a piece of rope. Now that room had been made, the oars could be worked properly, and course was resumed for the shore with the captain's body towing astern at the end of its line.

The corpse, floating upright, proved a difficult tow; men strained at the oars to move the boat, ever so slowly, determined to save both themselves and the body of their captain.

Bonner, in death as in life, proved mindful of the traditional captain's dictum that put the welfare of one's men first. After an hour of ever more difficult towing, the rudder was pulled right off the boat, and with its attached body, floated off astern. Willard Bonner, his last service done, disappeared in the mists forever.

An hour later, *Clayoquot* found her consort's last survivors and gathered them gently into the warm world of the living, leaving their shattered ship, and their dead captain and shipmates, in the cold clutches of the mighty river.

It was difficult to tell the injured from the healthy when *Charlottetown*'s people were put ashore at the Gaspé pier; men who seemed quite fit could suddenly develop the dreaded symptoms — retching, bringing up blood — of internal injuries due to the detonation of the ship's depth-charges. Telegraphist Edmund Robinson insisted on his fitness, only to collapse as he walked up the pier. Five days later he died in hospital, leaving fifty-four survivors from a ship's company of sixty-four.

The obviously fit, however, were hustled into barracks while the injured, for lack of better accommodation, were taken to the home of the base commandant, Commander Barry German, where they were laid out, still dripping water and oil, on the living-room carpet, and tended by Mrs. German. When transport arrived, they were taken off to the Hotel Dieu Hospital in nearby Gaspé village, where four later died. They were buried in a naval plot across the road from St. Paul's Anglican Church, following a moving funeral service conducted by the local vicar, the Reverend J. W. Wayman.

For those of us on the Goose Bay run, life went on serenely enough. All summer long and well into the fall we had plodded back and forth uneventfully between Quebec and Hamilton Inlet, passing north about Anticosti Island, quite oblivious of any activity on the south side, where Hartwig had set up shop. But for the Sydney-bound convoys, life continued to be unpleasant.

On September 15, Hartwig in *U-517* and Hoffmann in *U-165* carried out another combined attack, Hartwig surfacing inside the convoy to sink the Dutch *Saturnus* and the Norwegian *Inger Elizabeth* in a night foray, while Hoffmann torpedoed the Greek *Joannis* and the British *Essex Lance* the following morning. Although badly holed in the stern and abandoned by her crew, *Essex Lance* remained afloat. Boarded by the Fairmile *Q-052* and adjudged salvageable, she was towed to Quebec and repaired.

But this convoy had air cover as well as a couple of effective escort ships, and despite the atrocious sonar conditions they gave both U-boats a shaking up, firing full ten charge patterns on every possible contact. Hoffmann was glad to head for home following *U-165*'s mauling, but Hartwig, despite the damaging of his torpedo-firing gear, resolved to stick around and try to collect the extra tonnage he needed to qualify for his Knight's Cross. It took an awful lot of these tiny river steamers to add up to 80,000 tons.

Hartwig's luck, so phenomenal up until now, had finally run out. Although he hung around for a further three weeks, making a nuisance of himself, the only targets he could find were little river schooners not worth a torpedo, or neutrals, brightly lit and travelling independently, which he dared not touch. His cruise ended, not with a bang, but a whimper; after following a big and well-escorted convoy for days, he was forced to fire his last torpedoes at long range, and missed with all four. In dejection he turned for home at last, short of water and out of torpedoes and, saddest of all, with only 31,000 tons of shipping sunk to his credit.

But he had not reckoned with Nazi Germany's public relations experts. He arrived home to find his claims inflated to heroic proportions and to be greeted by brass bands and the coveted Knight's Cross bestowed by a beaming Führer.

With Hartwig's departure, the Gulf war to all intents and purposes was over, although we were not to know it at the time. Other U-boats ventured into the outer Gulf and even caused some losses; our old fat friend, the captain of the SS *Carolus*, finally got his on October 9 when his ancient ship was sunk by *U-69*. The wily skipper proved equal to the occasion, however. Although he had to flee his sinking ship without his trousers, he brought with him his money belt, stuffed with the proceeds of illicit liquor sales to thirsty Goose Bay construction crews, and was in his usual cheerful form when picked up by the corvette *Hepatica*.

Gradually the focus of attacks shifted from the Gulf out into the Cabot Strait; the SS *Waterton* was sunk there on October 11 by *U-106*, which was itself fortunate to survive an accurate attack by the armed yacht HMCS *Vison*, commanded by Lieutenant Bill Nicholson, RCNR. There were still U-boats in the Gulf right up until freeze-up; the frigate HMCS *Magog* was torpedoed off Cap Chat by *U-1223* on October 14, and as late as November 2, the SS *Fort Thompson* was torpedoed off Matane, but by that time most of us had returned to the serious business of Atlantic convoys, and the river war was over.

It is interesting to reflect on the subsequent careers of some of the protagonists. Hartwig, lucky to the last, was promptly attacked and brought to the surface on his very next cruise, to be put in the bag by a British destroyer. He sat out the rest of the war in a comfortable prison camp in Northern Ontario while his U-boat contemporaries were sunk in ever-increasing numbers. He was thus one of the few U-boat aces to survive the war and he returned to Germany as an officer in the new West German navy. As a German admiral and a NATO ally, he returned to visit Canada and be feted by the country to which he had once caused so much concern, and he now lives in pleasant retirement in West Germany.

Hoffmann, his Gulf partner, never made it back to Germany; his *U-165* was sunk in the Atlantic while homeward bound.

Some of our people didn't make it either. *Clayoquot*, the Bangor that had rescued *Charlottetown*'s survivors, was herself sunk on December 24 in the Halifax approaches.

For all of us in *Trail*, however, an even crueller loss was that of our "chummy ship", the corvette *Shawinigan*, torpedoed and lost with all hands while returning from a patrol in the Cabot Strait.

A Night to Remember

In retrospect, the Gulf war can be seen as a sideshow to the great debacle unfolding throughout the spring and summer along the southern coast of the United States, where U-boats were running wild through undefended shipping. In an even larger context, it was a flyspeck on the map of world events, where the Allies were sustaining a series of shattering blows brought on by the destruction of the U.S. battle fleet at Pearl Harbor. The total losses sustained — a handful of small and elderly merchantmen, a corvette, and an armed yacht — hardly counted in the overall totals of the Battle of the Atlantic, and the impending "invasion" of Canada, so fearfully predicted in the Quebec press of the time, amounted to the arrival of two German agents.

And yet . . . and yet . . .

German sailors *had* landed on the Labrador coast, the first armed enemy to violate Canadian territory since the Fenian raids of the previous century, and they had established an efficient weather station there which remained a permanent part of the landscape for more than thirty years.

A German U-boat, an enemy man-of-war, had penetrated the Canadian heartland to within a couple of hundred miles of a capital city and had sunk Canadian ships and killed Canadian seamen in full view of hundreds of Canadian onlookers. And, perhaps most humiliating of all, these enemy warships had operated for months at a time in Canadian waters, had wrought their damage, and had then been allowed to withdraw unscathed; despite plenty of near misses, not a single U-boat had been sunk in Gulf waters by Canadian sea or air forces.

On paper, it looked a pretty embarrassing defeat, but the truth is that the Gulf war was a moral victory for the Canadian government in general and the naval command in particular. Despite all the uproar from outraged members of Parliament and the outcry from Quebec newspapers, neither government nor the navy had lost sight of their primary objective to keep the men and materials flowing that were essential to sustain Britain at its time of greatest peril, and thus keep alight the flickering torch of freedom. If public pressure had succeeded in diverting urgently needed warships from the main theatre of the Atlantic battle, leaving the United States to flounder in the light of burning tankers along its eastern seaboard, and the great trans-Atlantic convoys had been stripped of their vital Canadian escort groups, it would have been a victory for the Nazi cause. The trickle of trade coming down the St. Lawrence, however valuable locally, was simply not worth the diversion of forces required to provide efficient escort. The sending of a few ocean escorts to the river theatre represented a compromise to appease Ottawa's critics. While still not doing an adequate job of protecting river trade, at least it was not enough to do serious harm to the really vital interests of the free world elsewhere.

Quebeckers were particularly annoyed by what they saw as unnecessary government secrecy and censorship regarding U-boat successes in the river; many sinkings were never acknowledged and details were sparse. What was not appreciated at the time was that U-boats were thus forced to signal their successes to Germany by wireless, which revealed their positions to shore stations. Even the barest details in the Canadian press could be of value to German naval command and could result in even more serious exploitation of an extremely vulnerable area—and the St. Lawrence's peculiar water mixture made it a very attractive operational area indeed for U-boats.

Yet perhaps the greatest effect of the war in the Gulf was that it helped end the traditional isolation of rural Quebec from events in the rest of Canada. Montreal, being a metropolis, had a sophisticated population that was close to, and vitally interested in, the affairs of the rest of Canada. But throughout rural Quebec in the early 1940s, English-speaking Canada was as remote as Europe, and its affairs were of no more interest. Rural Quebec in those days was dominated by a parochial clergy and, as we quickly appreciated when we began to operate there, it was the parish priest and not the mayor who had the final say on anything affecting his community, right down to the details of holding a dance or fielding a softball team. And despite pronouncements from its Montreal hierarchy, the church in Quebec had been firmly opposed to any participation in "the English foreign war", and openly connived to keep its young men from any form of war service.

The sinkings in their river, the window-rattling explosions and the oil-soaked survivors, had changed all that; the foreign war had somehow inexplicably moved onto their doorstep. Canadian sailors had been dying and Canadian ships been sinking for months, for years, but always that had happened off the coasts of some remote place like Nova Scotia, out of "English" ports like Sydney or Halifax. Now they were bringing dead men ashore in Gaspé and Matane, in Métis, and even in Quebec

City itself, and for the first time Canada's war was becoming Quebec's war, too.

After the river sinkings, the Chaudière regiment started to get recruits from the rural outback, and scores of young fellows eager to become sailors began to show up at HMCS *Montcalm*, the naval reserve division in Quebec City. All along the river, parish priests were starting to organize their communities into some form of war effort. Quebec — and Canada — would never be the same, for the Quiet Revolution was already under way.

A curious aspect of the war in the Gulf, however, was that its national significance, its social impact, and certainly its disasters, which the editorial writers seemed to feel so keenly as national humiliations, were all lost on those of us actually taking part. Embarrassing though it may be, it must be confessed that for most of us, especially those of us serving in ships detached from North Atlantic service, the summer in the St. Lawrence was a sort of idyllic holiday, a kind of picnic, with just enough action thrown in to keep things lively. Mostly it was the unfamiliar setting: the lovely green shoreline, the magnificent old city we were based in, the spectacular coast of northern Labrador with its awesome cliffs and towering icebergs.

Oh, the fogs and the slob ice and the crazy river traffic running without lights or sound signals brought on a few grey hairs, and the inadequate escorts and awkward convoys, together with poor radar and hopeless sonar conditions, made any sort of anti-submarine performance quite impossible, but we learned to live with that; at sea, everyone is a fatalist. And, after all, it was a kind of vacation from the real world, the real navy.

The lovely summer weather, the girls and gaiety of the Grande Allée and Dufferin Terrace, the short runs, the informality of the bases at Gaspé and Quebec City, a world away from the officious naval presence we were accustomed to in Halifax, all these added to the sense of holiday, of escape from the "real" war.

For most of us, it came to an end all too soon; the sunlit summer days, the bracing Labrador mornings, the fun-filled Château nights, became merely so many memories, to be relived as our corvettes dived into an Atlantic comber in the perpetual winter gale.

Most of us in the Newfoundland corvettes were already back at our old trade, screening Atlantic convoys, when the worst casualty of the whole Gulf war was sustained out in the Cabot Strait, where the last of the river U-boats were lingering before returning to base.

The SS *Caribou* was a medium-sized coastal passenger steamer, operating on a regular daily run between North Sydney in Nova Scotia's Cape Breton Island and Port aux Basques in Newfoundland, and after seventeen years of service she was a popular vessel and a local institution. Dutch-built, of just over 2200 tons displacement and 265 feet overall, she was the largest and fastest — at fifteen knots — ship on the Newfoundland service, and on the night of October 13, 1942, she left her pier at North Sydney with a complement of 191 passengers and 46 crew on board for the eight-hour crossing of the 96-mile-wide strait.

The *Caribou* departed at seven in the evening, sharp on time, and after the usual perfunctory "Lifeboat Stations" drill — few passengers seemed to have any idea of their proper station later on — she headed up toward Cape North in order to take evasive action, before settling on her course to Port aux Basques. The Bangor escort HMCS *Grandmère* took up screening station astern, working gradually across from quarter to quarter in what was then the approved screening position on a single-ship convoy.

Her asdic, the primitive Canadian set originally fitted, gave her a limited sonar capability, but she had no radar and therefore no capacity for detecting surfaced U-boats beyond the night vision of her lookouts. *Caribou* herself carried no radar, so the two vessels were virtually blind in the dark night as they groped their way across the dangerous strait; a disaster waiting to happen.

Early on the morning of the 14th, almost in the centre of the strait, a German U-boat, *U-69*, commanded by Ulrich Gräf, stumbled across the *Caribou*, quite by chance. Gräf had no idea a ferry route existed there, but fortune had put him in an ideal attacking position, broad on the starboard bow of what he misidentified, in the usual U-boat commander manner, as "a 6500 ton ship escorted by a two-stack[!] destroyer". Having inflated his target and its protector to properly heroic proportions, Gräf now set about the business of destroying them; just after 2:20 a.m. local time, he fired a torpedo at *Caribou* which struck her starboard side forty-three seconds later, blowing an enormous hole in her boiler-room amidships and destroying boats and upper-deck fittings immediately above. Mortally wounded, the stricken ship lurched heavily to starboard before rolling back to take on a heavy port list, filling rapidly through the gaping hole in her side.

Below decks, there were terrible scenes of panic as passengers fought to escape from the crowded public rooms, or from the staterooms where, only moments before, they had been sleeping soundly. The ship was obviously sinking rapidly; as frantic passengers fought their way along the narrow corridors they could hear beneath them the sounds of the sea rushing into their stricken vessel. The lights had gone out seconds after the torpedo struck, and the darkness and the danger made terrified people do mad, senseless things. One woman, reaching the upper deck, threw her tiny infant overside, then leaped after it into the sea. A fifteen-month-old baby, little Leonard Shier, was rescued three times by different rescuers and was the only one of the fifteen children on board to survive. Fear-crazed passengers sat obstinately in some lifeboats, preventing them from being turned out and launched; others cut boats adrift prematurely, without securing the drain plugs, allowing the boats to fill and sink. Some boats got away almost empty, others were so crowded that they capsized on meeting the water.

Yet in these terrible moments there were instances of calm bravery and selflessness. Men helped women into lifejackets; more than one gave up his lifebelt, and the opportunity of survival it represented, to a loved one or even a helpless stranger. Nursing Sister Margaret Brooke, RCNVR, of Ardath, Saskatchewan, was later awarded the Order of the British Empire for her efforts to save her drowning companion, Nursing Sister Agnes Wilkie, RCNVR, of Winnipeg.

The ship sank with frightening speed; in just over four minutes she was gone, carrying with her scores of screaming passengers and leaving dozens more struggling in the ice-cold water. After *Caribou* had disappeared, a desperate calm descended on the scene, broken only by the choking gasps of people battling to reach floating rafts, wreckage, or boats and stay alive. A seaman prayed aloud before drowning before the eyes of would-be rescuers in a lifeboat; groups of chilled survivors in a raft recited the Lord's Prayer, their thin chanting rising above the sounds of the sea and the terrible struggle on its surface. All through that dreadful night, the strong spiritual heritage of the Newfoundlanders shone through their fearful ordeal; it was the hymns the survivors sang that kept their spirits alive to greet the first light of dawn, and the sight of their escort vessel returning to rescue them.

For HMCS *Grandmère* it had been a night of horror and frustration. Closing *Caribou* after the torpedo struck, she had caught a glimpse of *U-69* on the surface, and had instantly altered round hard to starboard and increased to full speed in an attempt to ram. Gräf had seen her coming, however, and had taken *U-69* down in a steep spiralling dive, releasing a couple of *Pillenwerfer* bubble targets as he went to cloak his escape. Lieutenant J. Cuthbert, RCNR, had brought *Grandmère* in over the U-boat's wake and dropped a six-charge pattern by eye on the diving position, but in the difficult asdic conditions *Grandmère* was unable to maintain firm contact. In the long, anxious moments that followed as the little escort groped for her elusive enemy, Cuthbert dropped another dozen charges at medium, then deep, settings as he grasped at every contact, however momentary and fragile, but he never got firm contact, and he knew that with every passing minute his chances of doing so were growing slimmer. Disheartened and worn out by the fruitless search, *Grandmère* at first light turned to the task of rescuing *Caribou*'s survivors, strung out by now over miles of ocean.

She took on board 103 survivors, but two of them died on board. One of these deaths especially moved the hearts of everyone on board, naval crewmen and survivors alike; a tiny baby, blonde and blue-eyed and completely alone in the world, died in a sailor's arms while tears streamed down the seaman's face. Its identity was never learned.

In all, 136 men, women, and children died in the *Caribou* sinking, including 31 of her 46-man crew. The ship, like all Newfoundland ferries, past and present, was a family affair; Captain Ben Taverner's two sons, Stanley and Harold, sailed with him as first and third officers, respectively. All three were lost. Similarly, the sinking caused multiple losses in other Newfoundland families; the Coffins lost Elijah and Bert; the Gales,

George and Jerome; the Hanns, Clarence and Harry; the Stricklands, Garfield and Albert; the Thomases, Arthur and George. Most of the crewmen came from a handful of small Newfoundland communities, so that in hamlets like Channel, almost all the men in the community were wiped out by *Caribou*'s sinking.

In the tight-knit coastal communities of Newfoundland, the effects of the disaster were out of all proportion to the actual numbers lost, high though these were. The *Caribou* was more than a ship, more than a link with Canada and the outside world; she was a Newfoundland institution, and her loss was the heaviest blow sustained by the little colony throughout the whole of the Second World War.

The cruel circumstances in which so many of her people died, the deaths of so many women and children, even tiny babies, none of whom could be remotely connected with the conduct of the war, brought home to both Canadians and Newfoundlanders the barbarity of the war waged by U-boats against helpless merchant shipping. No longer could the Battle of the Atlantic be summed up in an accountant's balance sheet: so many thousand tons of shipping sunk, so many U-boats destroyed; after the *Caribou*, everyone in Canada realized, probably for the first time, the human tragedies that lay behind those simple statistics. No one on this side of the Atlantic would ever again identify submarine commanders like Ulrich Gräf, plying his grim trade in *U-69* among the grubby coasters off the Gulf coast, with the heroic figure of the dashing Günther Prien, stealing into the inner lair of the Royal Navy to sink a British battleship. For all of us engaged in it, the war at sea had always been a brutal business, but for most Canadians, accustomed to view it through newspaper accounts of distant heroics or impersonal balance sheets, the squalid realities had been filtered out through official releases and public relations glamour merchants.

The sinking of the *Caribou* ended all that. For all its insignificance to the war's worldwide power balance, in Canada and Newfoundland *Caribou*'s loss was the most significant sinking of the war.

As the U-boat tide receded from the Gulf, to wash about the rockbound coasts of Newfoundland, an even greater catastrophe at sea awaited the Canadian people, this time involving the loss of a Canadian naval frigate. The sinking of HMCS *Valleyfield*, only a few hours' steaming from her home port and in the close company of a whole escort group, surprised the nation and shocked the entire Canadian navy, although wartime censorship reduced discussion of its circumstances to scandalized whisperings and dark mutterings in wardroom and messdeck. The full details of the court of inquiry that investigated the circumstances of the loss of HMCS *Valleyfield* were only released to the public in the autumn of 1984.

Because of its elements of almost classical tragedy, and because it displayed, more clearly than almost any other incident of the war in Canada's waters, the agonizing and fateful decisions that must be made instantly by responsible men caught in the crunch of wartime circumstance, the story of the *Valleyfield* is the embodiment of the cruel sea war, worthy of being told in some detail.

DEATH IN THE MOONLIGHT

CURTAIN GOING UP

MIRROR-CALM under the bright moonlight, the sea stretched to infinity in every direction. To the northward, just over the horizon, a stately procession of enormous icebergs, islands of ice carved from the glaciers of western Greenland and cruising serenely on their months-long voyage to extinction in the vast reaches of the North Atlantic, raised their glittering pinnacles high in the pale moonlight, their passengers — seals, seabirds, and the occasional polar bear — growing restless as their dwindling argosies drifted ever southward.

To the east lay enormous fields of broken ice, "growlers" and "bergy bits" and long stretches of frozen slush, the outliers of the great ice-pack reaching down from the polar cap. The weight of billions of tons of ice oppressed the surface of the sea, damping the eternal Atlantic swell and reducing the whole of this patch of ocean in its lee to a huge millpond, unruffled and serene.

To the northwest, out of sight over the hazy horizon, lay the rocky ridges of Cape Race, the southeast corner of Newfoundland, the outermost tip of the land mass of North America and the traditional landfall of sailors voyaging from the Old World to the New. The Vikings had sailed this way a thousand years before, and Sir Humphrey Gilbert five hundred years later, in the wake of Cabot and the nameless adventurers of the European fishing fleets. The great circle route from the Channel to America's busy seaports passed just southward, the westbound track followed by the crack express liners of the Atlantic Ferry. All the great names, the fabled ships, of the western ocean had travelled this way, a smudge of smoke by day, long lines of glittering lights by night: the *Great Eastern* and the *City of Paris*, the *Kaiser Wilhelm der Grosse* and *Leviathan*, and the peerless *Mauretania* herself, churning these waters with their enormous screws. The riven hulk of the *Titanic* lay on the seabed a few score miles to the eastward, and passengers on the *Normandie* and the *Queen Mary*, strolling their midnight decks, had glimpsed the loom of the Cape Race light in the northern sky as their opulent floating hotels raced westward for New York.

But wartime had emptied these busy seas; ships travelled in convoy, and Cape Race was surrounded by empty ocean, broken only occasionally by salt-stained frigates, corvettes, and a few elderly destroyers bound northward for St. John's after an Atlantic crossing. On this night the sea lay empty and silent, bathed in pale moonlight, a faint mist softening the horizon, muffling the oily glint of the freezing water. Hushed and expectant, the floodlit stage awaited the entrance of the principals, for this was to be the scene of a dramatic encounter, a tragedy in two acts. Young men by the score were soon to die here, in this empty waste; the events to be played out in this moonlit theatre would change the lives of hundreds now asleep in the darkened land to the westward. Half a century later and half a world away men would still recall, with sadness and horror, the roles they played upon this unlikely stage, on this unforgettable night.

The date: May 6, 1944. The place: off the coast of the Avalon Peninsula, 150 miles southeast of Cape Race. It was an hour before midnight, local time, and the curtain was going up.

To the northward, something moved in the wan moonlight, breaking the silvered mirror of the sea. Sleek and sinister in the white light, the submarine glided smoothly onto centre stage, her trimmed-down hull barely awash, the V-shaped ripple of her bow wave animating the silent seascape. In her blunt ugliness, her sea-worn conning-tower and gun platform weeping with rust, she looked exactly what she was: a sea-beast ranging for prey. She was Unterseeboot *U-548*, commanded by Kapitänleutnant Eberhard Zimmermann, and she had arrived at this fateful rendezvous by a series of mischances and miscalculations.

U-548 was not the standard Type VII boat which formed the backbone of the German undersea fleet, and which had been turned out in its hundreds — 691 to be exact — since the middle 1930s. Rather, she was of a larger and newly developed type, the IXc, which represented a considerable technological advance on the older models, but like them she was still a "submersible", designed to attack on or near the surface, rather than a true submarine capable of operating submerged indefinitely. She was fitted with torpedo tubes in the stern as well as the conventional four in the bows, and she still had a complement of twenty-two torpedoes on board, having wasted one of them in a bungled attack the previous day. In addition to the conventional torpedo which exploded on contact with a target, she carried the new acoustic model, the "Gnat", which could be fired in the general direction of a selected target and then allowed to "home" with its sensitive microphones on the propeller noises of its victim. Built and in commission for nearly eighteen months, she was commanded by a seasoned officer and manned by an experienced crew, and more or less represented "the state of the art" of the German submarine branch after five hard years of sea warfare.

Zimmermann had been on his present patrol for about six weeks, and had drawn a complete blank. He had narrowly escaped attack only a few days before when, surfacing at dusk to ventilate the boat and take stock of his surroundings, he had found himself right below a large four-engined aircraft. A crash-dive had taken him to safety.

He had been continually forced to dive and take avoiding action while patrolling off the Newfoundland coast by various warships, and he had been plagued from the beginning by the presence of floating ice, which forced him to proceed much of the time well below the periscope depth he would have preferred. This made each surfacing a most anxious operation.

But most frustrating of all the circumstances that beset Zimmermann and *U-548* were the series of miscalculations that affected every aspect of the patrol. For one thing, he was almost always unsure of his position. In addition to the normal difficulties of navigating below the surface for long periods of time, the weather, during his sporadic visits to the surface, had almost invariably been overcast, foggy, or hazy, making celestial navigation all but impossible, and the coastal beacons were operated, in wartime, only when Allied shipping was in the vicinity. An attempt to use his radio direction-finder to fix his position was an utter failure; all the American commercial stations, Zimmermann noted bitterly in his log, "seemed to have changed their frequencies". The Kriegsmarine had thoughtfully furnished him with a list of U.S. radio stations, but, like much other information it had given him, it was incorrect and quite useless.

A few days earlier, however, he had been able to establish his position accurately for one of the few times on his cruise when he discovered the little Newfoundland coastal town of Baccalieu with all its lights blazing in defiance of wartime blackout regulations. The port was lit up "as if it were in peacetime", Zimmermann noted with considerable satisfaction, but after that *U-548* seemed to have operated largely by guess and by God. Whenever Zimmermann was able to obtain a fleeting check on his position, it was usually quite far from where he had thought himself to be, and he complained bitterly in his log about the strong current, but was unable to determine whether he was being set southwesterly or northeasterly.

Zimmermann's entire patrol seemed to have been founded on a miscalculation. It was difficult to believe that after five years of war Admiral Dönitz and his U-boat high command should have been ignorant of shipping routes off the Atlantic coast of North America, but the fact remained that *U-548* had been dispatched to patrol off the east coast of Newfoundland, at the height of the iceberg season, to seek out commercial shipping, which never operated within hundreds of miles of the area. Specifically, Zimmermann set out to hunt for merchantmen off the port of St. John's, which not only was avoided by almost all merchant shipping but was a principal base for the anti-submarine ships and aircraft that were the main danger to patrolling U-boats. All unknowing, *U-548* had strayed to the very threshold of the lions' den.

After a number of close encounters, the reality of his situation seemed to have been brought home to Zimmermann; on May 3 he noted in his log that "St. John's is probably a destroyer escort base", and because of this, as well as the ice, the heavy patrolling by "destroyers", the difficult visibility, and the lack of steamer traffic, he decided to move from the Cape Spear area, where he had spent such a difficult time, to a patrol further south, where he hoped to find some merchantmen for his torpedoes.

A surface vessel, which he classified as an American destroyer escort but which was almost certainly a British or Canadian frigate, had been encountered and cautiously closed. But the torpedo he had fired at her had missed, one of his diesel engines had emitted clouds of black smoke during the surface hunt, and he had been forced to take refuge beneath the surface in baffled frustration, after exchanging fire with a four-engined aircraft that suddenly appeared on the scene.

A remarkable aspect of *U-548*'s operations, as revealed in her war diary, was the difficulty U-boat commanders seemed to have, after five years of intensive warfare, in accurately identifying the Allied ships and aircraft that were their principal antagonists. Zimmermann classified all single-funnelled escorts encountered as "United States destroyer escorts", despite the fact that comparatively few such vessels operated in the area, compared with the enormous preponderance of single-funnelled frigates and corvettes of the British and Canadian navies. On May 3 he reported encountering a "Sunderland" aircraft, despite the fact these enormous British flying boats operated only on the eastern side of the Atlantic, and bore little resemblance to the Canso amphibian which was almost certainly what had flown over *U-548*.

On the evening of May 6, *U-548* received a wireless message from its headquarters in Germany: "Zimmermann, for Commander: Daughter born 4 May. Mother and daughter well. Congratulations. Admiral Commanding U-Boats."

So Zimmermann was a father. It was almost the only accurate information *U-548* had received from its operational authority.

What Zimmermann could not know was that his signals to his operational headquarters in Germany, and theirs to him, were being intercepted and read by staff officers at the British Admiralty in London. British code-breakers had cracked the "Ultra" secret and were reading German signals as quickly and accurately as the German forces for whom they were intended. Naval authorities in Newfoundland were aware of Zimmermann's presence; the aircraft that had forced him to crash-dive had been sent to look for him. They knew of his move to a new patrol ground, and they dispatched two corvettes of Escort Group W-2, HMCS *Timmins* and *Agassiz*, to hunt him down. At 1630 hours on the afternoon of May 6, Flag Officer, Newfoundland, made a general signal to all ships warning of the presence of a U-boat operating off the Avalon Peninsula in the vicinity of Cape Race, and giving the position of the ships of W-2 searching for it. The rust-streaked conning-tower shining wetly in the frosty moonlight was already being plotted in operations rooms on both sides of the Atlantic, and engaging the attention of eager young officers in chart-rooms at sea and in airfield briefing-rooms ashore.

Far to the southward, the signal was taken in by all the ships of Escort Group C-1, homeward bound for St. John's after escorting a westbound convoy. Four corvettes and a frigate of the Royal Canadian Navy, they had turned over their escort duties to a relief group early in the afternoon and were now steering northward on a direct course for St. John's at a speed of 13 knots. The U-boat report was in the signal log on the bridge of each ship, and officers coming on duty for the dog-watches had read it as they flipped through the latest messages to brief themselves before taking over the watch, but beyond that it received little attention. At sea, everyone in the escort groups had grown accustomed to warnings of U-boats which were never seen; the Atlantic was vast, and one U-boat more or less in a general area was "no sweat". Some other group had been told off to hunt the thing, so it was no responsibility of C-1's.

But there was more to it than that. "Channel Fever", the euphoria peculiar to homecoming sailors inward bound and already looking forward with eager anticipation to the delights of the shore, had C-1 firmly in its grip. Its men had left their responsibilities behind when they departed from the convoy. They had endured, with what patience they could muster, the program of group manoeuvres and exercises their Royal Navy senior officer had put them through — firing guns and rockets to order, exercising depth-charge crews, streaming and recovering Counter-Acoustical Torpedo gear — in mid-afternoon, and had accepted the necessity, in the exceptional visibility conditions prevailing, for adopting a group zigzag in order to present a difficult target for any enemy encountered, but nobody was really taking the U-boat threat seriously. Like a pack of schoolboys awaiting the classroom bell that would end the last day of school, the men of Escort Group C-1 went about their duties with at least half of their thoughts on their imminent homecoming a few short hours hence.

They ploughed through the shimmering sea in a long line abreast, *Valleyfield*, the senior ship, in the centre with the corvettes *Halifax* and *Frontenac* keeping station on the port beam, and *Giffard* and *Edmundston* to starboard, each ship 3000 yards from the next. On each bridge, watch-keeping officers kept a careful eye on the clock, as well as on the sea ahead, for they were zigzagging according to Admiralty pattern No. 10, which called for drastic alterations of course at varying intervals of time, making it impossible for any shadowing U-boat to line up its target for a torpedo attack. What complicated the problem of keeping good station was the floating ice, which the group began to encounter in mid-afternoon and which grew progressively thicker as they drove north. The "slob" ice and slush, rotten and waterlogged, were no danger to the thin steel hulls of the warships, but there was a sprinkling of heavier, bigger chunks — "growlers" and "bergy bits" which were dangerous — and here and there, scattered on the horizon, were full-fledged icebergs, towering mountains of ice which awed the most light-headed lookout. Keeping station under such conditions was by no means an easy matter for the harassed watch-keepers of C-1, and there was, accordingly, a collective sigh of relief when, at 2030, a signal from the senior officer cancelled the zigzag, leaving everyone free to steer a straight course and keep a watchful eye straight ahead.

Two hours later, the group passed through the last floating ice and emerged into a clear, mirror-like sea, ideal conditions for submarine attack, but the zigzag was not resumed. Steering a straight course meant an earlier arrival in port, and watch-keepers joked that their senior officer, Commander J. Byron, DSC, RN, was anxious to arrive in time for a cocktail party next evening, but the truth was that Byron, exhausted by nearly forty hours on the bridge, was asleep, and nobody thought it worth while to wake him.

It was the first link in a chain of circumstances that would end in disaster.

Valleyfield was completing her first trip as senior officer's ship. Commander Byron of the Royal Navy, nicknamed "The Brain", was the only British officer in the group, having transferred to her from the destroyer HMCS *Assiniboine* when the latter was delayed for repairs. Named for the Quebec town on the banks of Lake St. Francis, *Valleyfield* had been launched at Morton Drydock Company in Quebec City in July 1943, and commissioned on December 7 after running her trials in an ice-covered St. Lawrence. An ice-breaker had finally been required to carve a path through the ice to enable her and a little convoy of other recently completed ships — HMCS *Lindsay*, a corvette, *St. John*, a frigate, and the Royal Navy Algerine HMS *Postillion* — to escape into the ice-free Atlantic. She had worked up at St. Margaret's Bay and Bermuda before sailing on operations in February 1944, and by now, three months later, she had experienced a variety of assignments and was settling into harness as an accomplished mid-ocean escort on the Newfy-Derry "milk run", screening convoys in both directions from bases in St. John's and Londonderry.

She was a typical example of the highly successful River-class frigate that had evolved from the smaller corvette; just over three hundred feet overall, twin screw with a speed of 20 knots and great endurance, she carried two four-inch guns as surface armament and a large and varied range of anti-submarine and anti-aircraft weapons. She was commanded by a former Merchant Service officer, Lieutenant-Commander Dermot T. English, RCNR, who had formerly commanded the Bangor minesweeper HMCS *Mulgrave*. He had brought with him to his new command another officer from the *Mulgrave*, Lieutenant Ian Tate, RCNVR, and it was Lieutenant Tate who took over the frigate's bridge at 2000, with Lieutenant Cashman Mason, RCNVR, the ship's gunnery officer, as second officer of the watch. Both Byron and English had left the bridge at the turn of the watch, having been worn out by two days and nights of fog before leaving the convoy. They had been responsible for the safety of convoy ONM 234 ever since they had joined as escort south of Ireland, eleven days before. Now, relieved of their responsibility and with clear sailing for St. John's, only a few hours away, both sought some much-needed sleep, the senior officer in the captain's cabin and the captain in the chart-room bunk, his sea-berth. Responsibility for the safety of the group was now in the hands of the watch-keepers in each ship, and in *Valleyfield* there were problems.

To begin with, there was the ice; both officers were concerned with the amount of dangerous-looking floes about and were aware of the need for the lookouts in each wing of the bridge to keep a sharp watch over their sectors, to supplement that kept by themselves. But more worrisome was the poor performance of the ship's radar, a new and sensitive set requiring a high degree of sophisticated maintenance, a level beyond that of the operators *Valleyfield* carried. Accustomed to a simpler, more rugged machine, the operators had continual difficulty in regulating and adjusting the new RX/C equipment fitted in *Valleyfield*. Sighting a large iceberg ahead of the ship, and noting that it had not been reported by the radar operators, Lieutenant Tate called down the voice-pipe to the radar office to ask for a check on the berg's bearing. The operator reported that he could distinguish no echo on that bearing, but in any event the many bergy bits floating about the ship had cluttered the screen with so many echoes it was difficult to distinguish any one object. Disgusted with the set, which had proved a constant headache, Tate had the operator switch off the troublesome machine and activate the venerable SW1C set for watch-keeping.

Valleyfield was now dependent for detection of surface objects on the eyesight of her lookouts, with the questionable support of a primitive set dating from radar's Stone Age. On her port beam the corvette *Frontenac*'s radar set had been unserviceable for days, so that two out of the five ships, and those two in the heart of the group, were to all intents and purposes without radar coverage. It was another link in what was to be a fatal chain of circumstances.

However, radar coverage by the remaining ships was effective on either flank. At 2100 the corvette *Edmundston*, out on the extreme starboard wing, detected two targets ahead, and moments later *Giffard* also reported the surface objects on the starboard bow at a distance of three miles. These proved to be the corvettes *Timmins* and *Agassiz* carrying out an anti-submarine sweep for the U-boat reported in the area. *Timmins* flashed her running lights briefly to indicate her position and course, and the two groups, C-1 and W-2, passed each other at a safe distance on opposite courses.

At 2240 the C-1 group detected an aircraft by radar, the target closing rapidly from the starboard beam. It was identified as an RCAF Canso by *Giffard*, and as it flew low over the group it switched on its powerful Leigh light, briefly illuminating the corvette *Halifax* in its bright glare. Satisfied that the "blip" on the port side was a corvette and not a shadowing U-boat, the Canso switched off its light and flew off westward; it, too, was searching for *U-548*.

On the bridges of the escort ships, the watch-keepers muttered maledictions after the disappearing plane; pilots who illuminated "friendly" ships could often expect a few "friendly" bursts of tracer in return, but in this instance it was a bright moonlit night, home port was only just over the horizon, and everyone on the duty watch was in a good mood.

The ships of C-1 were approaching the general area within which the U-boat had been reported, confident of their own invulnerability. They were, after all, anti-submarine ships, travelling in close company, more than a match for any wandering U-boat. They were the hunters of U-boats, not their prey, and this frame of mind conditioned the attitude of every man in the group.

As mentioned earlier, that afternoon they had exercised in

streaming their Counter-Acoustic Torpedo equipment, known simply as CAT gear. This consisted of a pair of metal pipes a few feet long, clamped parallel to each other a fraction of an inch apart, streamed at the end of a wire bridle and towed astern of the ship. The pipe sections vibrated, making a great deal of underwater noise which sounded something like a power saw, and this underwater noise attracted German acoustic torpedoes ("Gnats") and prevented them from homing on the propeller noise that was their intended target. Escort vessels were being attacked by this new weapon — the destroyer *St. Croix*, the frigate *Itchen*, and the corvette *Polyanthus* had been lost to Gnats in a single convoy battle the previous year — and the rule for escorts operating near a suspected U-boat was that they should either stream their CAT gear or reduce speed to six knots or less, at which speeds their propeller noise was insufficient to attract the Gnat.

But the CAT gear noise was loud enough to hamper the asdic operators when sweeping on beam bearings, and was a negative factor even on an efficient sweep ahead or on bow bearings, so that ships seldom streamed their CAT except when a U-boat was known to be near.

And so it was that the five ships of C-1 entered the signalled U-boat operating area steaming at 13 knots, with CAT gear secured inboard, steering a straight course with no zigzag over a mirror-smooth sea, under a bright moon and clear sky, with two adjacent ships in the centre of the group without operational radar, their senior officer sunk in exhausted sleep and their officers and men already preoccupied with their imminent arrival in home port. The chain of circumstances was now complete and the group was already locked into a fatal pattern, steaming directly towards *U-548*.

Zimmermann had been proceeding cautiously on the surface since dusk at 2040 and steering south toward the outer limit of his patrol area, where he hoped to find himself closer to the convoy routes and the prey which had so far eluded him. He was relieved to find himself moving into a relatively ice-free area; the previous night he had expended much time and energy in a careful stalk of three large shadows, sighted on the horizon, which after a painstakingly careful approach proved to be three icebergs. It had all been very embarrassing, and he was pleased that at the moment there seemed to be no such large ice in the near vicinity. Early that afternoon, while lying submerged, he had watched from his periscope while the corvettes *Timmins* and *Agassiz*, which he had mistakenly identified as ''U.S. destroyer-escorts'', had swept past him during the course of their search, and he had heard, though not sighted, an aircraft passing over at some distance.

Shortly after surfacing at dusk, he had observed that a light mist and a quarter overcast were limiting visibility somewhat, although the moon remained very bright, and two hours later stratus cloud had moved in, limiting visibility still further. He had been greatly elated to receive the signal from U-boat headquarters, apparently from Admiral Dönitz himself, announcing the birth of his daughter, his first child, and the spirits of both crew and commander were lifted by this indication of their admiral's personal interest in *U-548*. With almost a full complement of torpedoes, and a captain and crew yearning to use them, *U-548* motored slowly southward, directly into the path of C-1.

The two principals, and their supporting casts, were now on stage: *Valleyfield*, with her attendant corvettes, steaming north at 13 knots, entering from the left, and *U-548*, trimmed down so that only her conning-tower and upper casing showed above the unruffled surface, and motoring southward at six knots, entering on the opposite side. The stage was set and brilliantly lit, the players in their places; at any moment contact would be made and the play, a tragedy, would begin. It was half an hour before midnight, and Death was waiting in the wings.

ILL-MET BY MOONLIGHT

HIS MAJESTY'S CANADIAN SHIP *Valleyfield* was a happy ship. Apart from Commander Byron, the senior officer, and five British ratings also from the Royal Navy, the rest of her complement, 14 officers and 143 men, were Canadians, almost all of them volunteer reservists. There was nothing unusual about this, Canada's few professional naval officers and men being fully occupied in operating the training and operational establishments ashore and the handful of larger warships that the Royal Canadian Navy possessed. The hundreds of ships that made up Canada's contribution to the Battle of the Atlantic were manned almost entirely by reservists.

In *Valleyfield* there were many junior seamen, stokers, and communications ratings for whom the frigate was their first seagoing ship, and whose sea time was limited to the three months in which the ship had been operational. But there was a large proportion of experienced petty officers, leading hands, and other senior personnel, as well as officers, to leaven the mixture, and to add competence and confidence to a ship's company that had stabilized quickly. These officers and men were veterans of corvettes and minesweepers, the little ships that were the backbone of the North Atlantic escort forces. Their hard-won experience and expertise had carried the ship through its earliest days, and blended with the youth — the average age of Canada's volunteer sailors was twenty-two — and enthusiasm of "first-trippers" to make up a contented and competent ship's company.

On this May evening, the messdecks below were abuzz with cheerful activity as off-duty watchmen prepared themselves for arrival in St. John's next morning and relaxed after another westward convoy crossing. There had even been an "amateur hour" program during the dog-watches over the ship's internal loudspeaker system. As well as the usual Glenn Miller and Tommy Dorsey records played in response to requests from individual crewmen, there had been special performances by mouth-organists and struggling guitarists among the ship's company to entertain their shipmates. A special feature had been the recitation of doggerel verse by Bert Ward, a bearded signalman, and everyone had been in good spirits when the ship piped down and messdecks darkened after the last dog-watch ended at 2000.

Muffled in sheepskin-lined watch coats or hooded duffle coats, the signalmen and lookouts on *Valleyfield*'s bridge stamped the biting cold from their feet as they peered into the moonlit night, while Lieutenants Tate and Mason kept their vigil on the raised compass platform in the bridge centre. The radar operators rotated their masthead antenna, the "plumber's nightmare" characteristic of the ancient SW1C set, and peered hopefully at its cluttered green screen, while in their tiny cabinet in the forepart of the bridge the asdic operators searched beneath the calm sea for any submerged submarine or other underwater object. At a combined closing speed of something over twenty miles an hour, still unaware of each other, frigate and submarine rushed headlong toward certain collision.

It was Zimmermann himself, in the conning-tower of *U-548*, who made the initial sighting, a pale shadow in the moonlight ahead, fine on his port bow. He was alarmed by the rapidity with which the target was closing, and crash-dived before even his trimmed-down hull might become visible to the onrushing ship. To gain time to prepare an attack, he put the U-boat on a parallel course and increased to full speed. He now had the opportunity to study the target more closely through his periscope; it was, he decided, "clearly recognizable as a United States destroyer escort"; his difficulty in identifying Allied warships was to persist to the end. He had sounded action stations as he dived, and all the U-boat's tubes were now prepared for underwater firing, their crews standing by while Zimmermann examined his target. His own alteration of course had given him the illusion that his prey was zigzagging, but he was able to ascertain her "mean" course accurately enough as true north, and to reckon her speed at 14 knots, an error of only one knot; a commendable performance for a snap assessment through a periscope of a dangerous and fast-approaching enemy.

Putting *U-548* on a slightly converging course, Zimmermann now closed in for the kill. The time was 2335.

Zimmermann had made his sighting at something like three nautical miles and now, as the ships of C-1 closed the range, his periscope, barely awash in the smooth sea, would have been virtually undetectable even had *Valleyfield*'s centimetric radar set been operational. Asdic operating conditions gave C-1's sonar sets a practical range of approximately 3000 yards that night, so the U-boat was still well beyond the limits of underwater asdic detection. *U-548* had achieved the ultimate submariner's goal as the undetected and undetectable stalker of his selected victim.

Yet there were unpleasant surprises ahead for Zimmermann.

Until now, he had failed to detect any ships in company, considering his intended prey as an isolated U.S. destroyer escort on passage. Had he been aware that he was tackling not a single ship but an entire escort group in spread formation, he would never have been so rash as to attempt an attack, particularly from right ahead in the group's path. Accordingly he was shattered when the U-boat's hydrophone operator suddenly called out that there were high-speed propeller noises to port and, a moment later, similar frightening sounds to starboard. In consternation, Zimmermann rotated his periscope right around the horizon, but its limited range, from just above the surface, revealed nothing. He had blundered into something of a hornet's nest, but his nerve never failed him. Staying rock-steady on the attack course he had selected, and paying no heed to the rapidly approaching propellers whose amplified din now filled the U-boat, he waited until the target range closed to 1500 metres. At 2332 exactly he fired a T 5, a "*Zaukönig*" or acoustic homing torpedo, at *Valleyfield*, set to run at a depth of four metres and aimed at her port bow. Immediately after firing, he put the U-boat into a steep diving turn to starboard, hoping to go deep and evade the onrushing warships whose propeller noises could now be heard on all sides. *Valleyfield*, and most of her young sailors, had only seconds to live.

Aboard the doomed ship, the unvarying routine of a warship at sea went on as always, day or night. The watch below had just been "shaken", the usual half-hour notice for sleeping crewmen to bestir themselves and dress to go on watch. The duty bosun's mate had made his way through the darkened messdecks, where rows of hammocks swayed gently to the motion of the ship, slapping the sagging bottom of a "mick" here, shaking a sleeper's shoulder there, murmuring the dreaded

"Wakey! Wakey!" loud enough to rouse the men of the next duty watch without disturbing the slumber of the others still asleep all about them. Many crewmen were sleeping, as always at sea, more or less fully dressed except for boots and coats, ready for any emergency, but with the ship due to berth in St. John's in a few hours, quite a few were sleeping in more comfortable "shoreside fashion", dressed only in underwear shorts. In the cramped petty officers' mess, Yeoman Irving Kaplan, the senior signal rating onboard, was asleep on the cushioned locker top that ran down one side of the mess, fully dressed in a warmly padded zip-up "zoot suit", with his heavy naval-pattern lifejacket on top of that, ready for any emergency call that might summon him to the bridge. By contrast, Coder Ed Munro, just clambering out of his hammock and sleepily preparing to go on watch at midnight in the wireless office, was dressed only in shorts as he fumbled for his shirt and trousers.

In the noisy clamour of the engine room, the senior watch-keeping petty officer wrote up his log in the bright glare of the overhead lights, while his artificers moved about the whirling, gleaming machinery of their two monstrous charges, checking bearings and oil levels and thinking ahead to the haven of quiet and sleep that awaited them in their darkened messdeck, less than half an hour from now. Near by, in the searing heat of the boiler-rooms, the duty stokers wiped the sweat from their brows as they kept a watchful eye on the all-important gauges that monitored the pressures and temperatures that drove the ship onward.

On the bridge, too, the pervasive restlessness that precedes a change of watch was making itself manifest; lookouts shuffled their numbed feet, drew themselves deeper into the recesses of their hooded watch coats as they swept their binoculars through their assigned arc of horizon for the hundredth time, empty of everything save misty, moon-bright sea. Hands thrust into pockets, the duty signalman stumped in heavy seaboots across the rear of the bridge, watchful for any flickering signal lamp from the unseen ships reaching to the horizon on either side.

On the compass platform, Lieutenant Mason was "driving", as the officers jokingly called it, positioned above the voice-pipes at the gyro compass binnacle and passing orders to the quartermaster at the wheel on the deck below him. Lieutenant Tate, who shared the watch and alternated with him at the conning position, was free at the moment to supervise the radar and sonar searches and the vigilance of the bridge lookouts, as well as maintaining a general lookout himself.

About half an hour before midnight, he noticed that the "captain's pointer" on the compass, which indicated the direction in which the asdic was transmitting, had steadied on a bearing at "Red 60", broad on the port bow. Apparently the asdic operator was investigating something on that bearing and, curious to know what it might be, Tate, who was the ship's anti-submarine officer, switched on the bridge loudspeaker, which amplified whatever the operator could hear.

The operator had momentarily stopped the set's asdic transmissions in order to listen to something — something off *Valleyfield*'s port bow. And now, as they too craned to listen, everyone on the bridge could hear it also, magnified by the loudspeaker beside them. It was a curious sound, like nothing any of them had ever heard before: a soft, quick ticking, like that of a watch, but much faster, almost a hum. Swiftly, smoothly, as inevitable and irrevocable as Time itself, Death rushing upon them!

"Investigate from 250 degrees to 290 degrees," Tate called through the asdic voice-pipe, giving the set an arc to sweep through that would search along the bearing of the strange underwater noise, but even before the operator could acknowledge the order, the torpedo struck.

"WHAM!"

The shattering crash of the explosion, on the port side just abaft the bridge, sent a great cloud of flame, water, and steam towering high above the ship into the pale moonlight. The impact shook the frigate from stem to stern, tumbling men from bunks and locker tops, throwing watch-keepers off their feet, wrenching and breaking the fabric of the ship and numbing the minds of her crewmen with its explosive shock, and yet the ingrained discipline and ordered routine of the ship, the pulse of life that animates every naval vessel, still continued to function. On the bridge, Lieutenant Mason reached for the emergency bell push beside the binnacle and set the alarm bells pealing throughout the ship, summoning all hands to their action stations and awakening not a few who had slept soundly even through the din of the explosion. Lieutenant Tate scrambled across the bridge to the engine-room voice-pipe, hoping to inform the stokers and artificers of what had happened and to clear everyone out of the lower-deck spaces, but he was a second too late; even as he jabbed at the button of the call bell, the ship's power failed and all her lights went out, all her bells fell silent. *Valleyfield* was mortally wounded, and one by one her vital functions ceased.

The torpedo had struck the ship in No. 2 boiler-room, killing the stokers there instantly and rupturing the main fuel tanks; already the thick, syrupy bunker oil was welling into the sea, to be turned by the freezing cold into a thick, viscous, tar-like scum that quickly spread out over the calm surface. The ship began to break apart at the point of explosion, the mainmast staggering drunkenly, waving a wild pattern against the pale sky before its standing rigging parted, and it fell with a crash over the side. The forward part of the ship, fo'c'sle and bridge, separated from the after half with a rending screech, and listed rapidly over to starboard as its lower spaces were filled by the inrushing sea; on the bridge the watch-keepers could only hold on as best they could, numbed by shock and deafened by the frightful din of escaping steam and the shriek of tortured, tearing metal. Lieutenant Tate, clutching the binnacle on the sharply listing compass platform, was suddenly aware of the navigator, Lieutenant Warren, and the captain, Lieutenant-Commander English, on the bridge beside him; both had come up from the chart-room on the deck below.

Lieutenant-Commander English wasted no time. Taking in the situation at a glance, he leaned over the rear bridge dodger and shouted to the dark knot of men scrambling up to the boat-deck: "Man boats and Carley floats!"

It was the last order given aboard *Valleyfield*, and it marked the end of her short life as a commissioned fighting ship; henceforward she was a mere hulk, a sinking wreck to be abandoned as quickly and expediently as possible. With each passing moment her forward portion listed more heavily to starboard and, as her fo'c'sle decks filled with the in-flooding sea, her open bridge end began to sink and her bows, slowly but surely, began to rise. She was starting to stand on end and, in the sealed-off messdecks, the last, terrible agonies of her trapped crewmen began.

On the bridge, Lieutenant Tate now noticed that the captain was wearing no lifebelt; he had, it appeared, thrust it upon some frightened crewman, frantic for a lifebelt, whom he had encountered on his way to the bridge. Ironically, Lieutenant-Commander English, always punctilious about the wearing of lifejackets at sea by everyone, on duty and off, now found himself the only man on the bridge of his sinking ship without a lifejacket. Tate sought to remedy the situation by offering his captain one of the Kisbee life-preservers that hung in brackets on the bridge dodger, a canvas-covered cork ring intended to be tossed quickly to anyone who fell overside. He and his captain fought desperately to remove the ring from its holder, but with no success; it was jammed and painted securely in its holder, and could not be budged. Like so much emergency equipment never used normally, it failed in its single moment of need.

"It's no good, sir," shouted Tate at last, "we'll never get this free. Better swim for it!" The captain had come to the same conclusion; as his stricken ship listed over still further, and it was obvious that nothing further could be done to save either her or any of her men who were not already on deck, he clambered over the bridge railing and, with Lieutenant Warren beside him, walked down the port side of the ship, now almost horizontal, toward the bright sea beyond. From the bilge keel, now fully exposed, they launched themselves into the freezing water and joined the cluster of gasping, struggling swimmers already spreading out from the doomed wreck.

Valleyfield was now going over so quickly that Lieutenant Tate, from his perch on the binnacle, was unable to follow his fellow officers down the port side. As the sea lapped over the starboard bridge dodger, he simply flung himself into it. The bows of the ship, standing on end, towered over him; for a moment he feared they might topple on him. Unable to swim clear, he found himself sucked down in the vortex as the vast mass of metal sank into the sea, and dragged him with it down into the icy depths. Encumbered by his heavy clothes, he struggled desperately, blindly, upward, and as the buoyancy of his lifejacket asserted itself, he won free from the suction of the sinking hulk and popped like a cork back to the surface.

Gasping for breath, he found himself only yards away from a floater net, a webbing of rope some twenty feet square, buoyed up by hundreds of cork floats and carried in open racks on the upper deck of all naval vessels for just such emergency use. A few strokes brought him to the net, where he was quickly joined by several other swimmers. The net kept them from sinking but left them immersed in the freezing sea up to their shoulders. It was obvious that they could not long survive, half awash on their perilous perch, but as the turbulence from the sinking bows subsided, Tate spotted a Carley float, already laden with men, floating a little distance away. Together with his fellow survivors, he swam from the floater net to the more solid safety of the Carley float, which now supported some twenty crewmen. Dangerously overloaded, the Carley raft was now barely afloat; some of the men it supported huddled, knee-deep in water, on the slatted wooden grating suspended in its centre, others sat astride the cork "doughnut" ring supporting it, their legs dangling in the sea, while the rest merely hung, semi-submerged, about its outer sides, clutching the lifeline that girdled the raft.

Like some of his fellow swimmers, Tate snapped the steel spring-hook that dangled at the end of a short lanyard from his lifebelt onto the Carley raft's lifeline to ensure he would not lose his hold, and from this temporary refuge he was able, for the first time, to look about him at the general situation.

The stern half of *Valleyfield* was still afloat; as the open forward portion rapidly flooded with the inrushing sea, it gradually sank, lifting the stern clear of the sea. The rudder appeared, then the screws, still turning slowly, gleaming wetly in the bright moonlight; as the shivering survivors watched in frozen fascination, their ship performed the last, terrible act of its death throes. Slowly, deliberately, to the accompaniment of bursting bulkheads, exploding boilers, and screaming crewmen, His Majesty's Canadian Ship *Valleyfield* stood on its end, her slim body, revealed now in all its gleaming beauty, poised for the final plunge.

Within that lovely hull the surging sea, exploding inwards with fearful force, was quenching the final agonies of the scores of trapped men, seamen as well as stokers and artificers, fighting desperately for their lives. But on her upper deck, now tilting perilously into the sky, another struggle had been fought and won; it was a victory, won at the cost of life itself, which would yet earn a chance of survival for all those other crewmen now floating in the sea.

Three torpedo ratings — Leading Seaman Donald Henry Brown, Ordinary Seaman David Edgar Brown, and Able Seaman Mervyn E. Woods — had made their way aft immediately after the torpedo had struck. Clutching at every handhold, and climbing upwards as the sinking hull tilted ever more sharply, the three seamen reached the quarterdeck and, working frantically, they set the ready-use depth-charges to "Safe" and withdrew the primers. This "pattern" of ten charges, always kept ready for instant firing, would have detonated the moment their hydrostatic pistols filled with water as the ship sank, and their explosion could have blown the stern section to pieces and killed every man in the water. None of the trio were ever seen again. They rode the wreck of the stern section through its final moments and were sucked down with it to the bottom, but their devotion to duty had won for their shipmates a chance for survival. It was a selfless sacrifice, one of many which ennobled *Valleyfield*'s final moments as men scrabbled and fought, each locked into his own selfish, desperate struggle for life.

A calcium flare, attached to one of the Kisbee life-rings and designed to illuminate on contact with the water, now ignited, its flickering brilliance adding an eerie aspect to the bright moonlit scene. The surface of the sea was covered with a thick layer of fuel oil from the ruptured bunkers, its heavy reek permeating everything.

In this viscous pool scores of swimmers, most supported by lifejackets but a few without, struggled to stay alive. All of them were drawn to the three Carley floats which bobbed, already heavy-laden, in the troubled water marking the grave of the sunken forward section of the frigate, and with every passing minute the rafts sank still lower under a growing burden of oil-soaked, gasping men, each fighting for a seat or a mere handhold on their oil-slicked sides.

Kaplan, the signal yeoman, was one such; he had already survived a series of circumstances that had killed many. He had managed to escape from the flooding petty officers' mess through a deck-head hatch and had walked up the side of the heavily listing ship to the gundeck, where he attempted, with three other men, to launch the Carley float. The heavy float could not be budged because of the impossible list to the ship, so it had been abandoned, and Kaplan had clambered onto the gun-shield of the forward four-inch mounting as the sea lapped over the gun platform. Abandoning his perch, Kaplan took to the water, and swam away from the ship to join Leading Seaman Guthrie, who was hanging on to a Kisbee life-ring. The two paddled desperately to get away from the sinking bow section, which reared high above and threatened to topple down and crush them. Kaplan had been forced to abandon the life-ring when its calcium flare ignited and began to burn him, but his lifejacket buoyed him up and enabled him to swim the considerable distance to the main group of survivors, where he was eventually to find a precarious seat on the supporting ring of a Carley float so heavily laden that he, like all his fellow survivors on the ring, was up to his waist in the icy water.

His thick "zoot suit" gave him ample protection, and he was fit enough to assist those around him. He helped several to find a place around the raft's ring, and clipped their lifejackets to the lifeline that hung from it in loops. One swimmer, unable to find space, simply clung to Kaplan's leg, while others hung on to the rope net that had been fastened to one side of the raft, and that now joined it to an adjacent Carley float.

One of those clinging to the net was the captain, Lieutenant-Commander English, who, without a lifejacket, was up to his shoulders in the water. Seeing his signal yeoman atop the raft, English called out to him: "Count the men!"

Kaplan accordingly began to do so, and counted twenty-two on or about the raft, but there were so many heads bobbing about close by and so many others massed in clusters or on pieces of wreckage that he could not get an accurate count, and rather than confuse the captain with an inaccurate total he kept silent. In the numbing cold of the oil-slicked sea, it was already becoming difficult to differentiate between the living, the dying, and the dead.

Of all those desperate, oil-soaked men, none were more vulnerable than Coder Ed Munro. When the torpedo struck, Munro had been standing beside his hammock in the communications mess, dressing to go on watch in the wireless office. The resultant explosion had wiped out his warm, sleepy world in the twinkling of an eye; Munro found himself, dressed only in his underwear shorts, in the sudden darkness of a sinking ship, the deck already tilting sharply under his feet and icy water surging over his ankles. Snatching up his lifejacket and buckling it about him as he moved, Munro managed to clamber out of the escape hatch onto the deck-head above and plunged into the sea that was already swallowing up the forward half of the ship. The chill of the 32-degrees-Fahrenheit water bit into his bare body, numbing mind and senses, so that he functioned like an automaton, driven by a blind instinct to survive. He swam desperately at first, to avoid being sucked down with the forward half of the ship, already beginning its final plunge to the bottom far below. Once clear, he found himself in a pool of oil littered with wreckage and floating debris of every kind.

There was a raft near by, and Munro made his way to it, joining the little huddle of men who fringed its sides, submerged to their shoulders and hanging on to the lifeline that was looped around the outer edge of the float. Numbed and chilled and covered with oil, he and his shipmates watched with horrified fascination as their ship, rearing high in the moonlight, began to slip beneath the glittering surface. Slowly, deliberately at first, then with ever-increasing rapidity as her overtaxed bulkheads gave way, she disappeared from sight, carrying with her the warm home and ordered world they all had known and the shipmates, dead and dying, of only a few minutes before.

On one of the rafts, someone began to sing: "For she's a jolly good fellow, for she's a jolly good fellow—" and everyone in earshot joined in. As *Valleyfield*'s pastel-painted hull slipped forever from mortal gaze, the thin voices of her shivering crewmen sang her requiem.

TRAGEDY, PART TWO

IMMEDIATELY after firing, Zimmermann had put his helm hard to starboard and taken *U-548* into a steep dive, turning sharply as she went. Levelling off at a safe depth, he shut off his electric motors and listened for the results of his attack.

He had not long to wait. Exactly three minutes and twelve seconds after the time of firing, as measured on his stopwatch, there came the unmistakable sounds of a hit: "a very loud, hollow-sounding detonation", as he noted in his log. There were no more propeller noises from the direction of *U-548*'s victim, only "violent break-up and cracking noises". Zimmermann could not know it, but he was listening to the sound of *Valleyfield* literally being torn in two.

The jubilation that filled every member of the U-boat's crew, as realization of their success spread throughout the boat, changed gradually to awe, as the frightful sounds of their victim's death-throes filled the submarine, amplified by the loudspeakers of the hydrophones. For what seemed an incredibly long period the submariners were deafened by a sustained roaring and hissing and cracking, as the inrushing sea drove the trapped air from the doomed frigate, and bulging bulkheads gave way under enormous pressure. The noise seemed to be coming closer, as if wreckage were showering down upon the submarine, and

Zimmermann got the impression that the shattered hull was sinking directly upon him, threatening to trap the U-boat under the weight of its victim. He got under way again, settling on a southwesterly course, and only seconds later — one minute and thirty-two seconds after the hit, according to his remorseless stopwatch — he heard the impact of "a large piece of debris" striking the sea bed close by. The sound Zimmermann heard, and dutifully recorded in *U-548*'s log, was the bow section of *Valleyfield* coming to rest on the bottom, bearing with it, dead or dying, most of the frigate's crew. The U-boat, now clear of any possible sinking wreckage, throttled back to "dead slow" for silent running.

On tiptoe, the killer stole from the scene, away from the crumpled body of his victim.

On the surface, the singing and the shouting had subsided; the numbed survivors clung to rafts and wreckage and prayed fervently for rescue, swift and soon. For a time, all movement ceased; the moon shone down on an oily sea, dotted with flotsam, with darker clots where men huddled about a Carley float or a large piece of wreckage, with here and there the winking light from a lifejacket torch, switched on by a sodden survivor. The stage was set now for the second act of the tragedy, and already the principal player was making an entrance.

Aboard the corvette *Giffard*, on *Valleyfield*'s starboard beam, the impending change of watch had brought the usual orderly stir and bustle below decks, and the routine checking of responsibilities by the off-going duty watch.

HMCS *Giffard* was not an especially happy ship. There was a tension between her commanding officer and the wardroom officers that inevitably pervaded the whole vessel, and it stemmed from the personality of her captain. Lieutenant-Commander Charles Petersen was one of a unique group of ex-merchant-navy officers serving in the Royal Canadian Naval Reserve known as "The China Coasters". These were seamen who had served in the British-officered Chinese Customs Service, or in merchant ships operating out of Chinese ports, and who had come to Canada's West Coast on the outbreak of war and been commissioned into the Royal Canadian Naval Reserve, to take command of the corvettes and frigates of the escort navy.

Most of them — George Hall, Howard Wallace, "Rafe" Barrett, and many others — went on to distinguished careers in Canada's navy; Tony Storrs became an admiral. But for a few of them the adjustment from handling coolie crews to commanding ships' companies of spirited young Canadian volunteers, who could be led but not driven, was too much to cope with. Certainly Petersen had found it difficult to entrust his young and, to his eyes, inexperienced officers with the authority and responsibility they were eager to assume. The resultant tensions only served to increase the burden of stress borne by *Giffard*'s already over-tense young captain.

He was sleeping now in his bunk below *Giffard*'s bridge, where both the officer of the watch and the coxswain, who was sharing the watch with him, swept the horizon with their binoculars, noting that all was clear ahead, before steadying their glasses on *Valleyfield*, their senior officer, to ensure that they were still in correct station. They could see her very plainly, every detail showing clearly in the moonlight — and then it happened. Suddenly, incredibly, an enormous white column of spray or steam, or both, towered high above the frigate, right amidships. Speechless, incredulous, they stared at that monstrous white column, now overtopping mast and funnel, and then, while they stared, white-faced and shaken, at the pillar now breaking up and dissipating into a shimmering cloud, they felt, as well as heard, the explosion.

"*Boom!*"

It was the sound of that explosion, more than the alarm buzzer of his voice-pipe, that brought *Giffard*'s captain, grim-faced and alert, to his bridge.

A capable and experienced officer, Petersen was none the less puzzled by the sound of the explosion, and by the report of his watch-keeping officer about the column of water and smoke he had seen erupt from *Valleyfield*'s side. Had the frigate sustained an engine-room explosion, or had a boiler exploded? Had she fired a "pattern", perhaps, or had a depth-charge been accidentally dropped at a shallow setting? *Giffard*'s young captain revolved the possibilities in his mind as the precious seconds ticked by. It was not until 2343 — three full minutes after he had heard the explosion — that Petersen, now growing alarmed, ordered *Giffard* to be put around on a course to close *Valleyfield*, and at the same time he began to call her on R/T, the ultra-high-frequency radio telephone that allowed the officers of one ship to communicate in plain language with other ships in company.

There was no response whatever, and, as Petersen's alarm grew, his radar operator reported, first, that *Valleyfield*'s "blip" on his screen was diminishing, and then, seconds later, that it had disappeared. Now deeply concerned, Petersen ordered his yeoman to attempt to contact *Valleyfield* visually, by sending her call letters on *Giffard*'s signalling-light projector, directed at the frigate's estimated position. There was no reply, no answering flash of light.

Her signal projector sending staccato flashes into the empty night, *Giffard* edged closer to *Valleyfield*'s last reported position, every officer and lookout on her bridge intently searching the glittering sea through binoculars. The anxious, urgent seconds ticked inexorably by, with nothing seen, nothing to show — and then, there it was! There! There! Far astern of where the frigate should have been, a light glowed and winked; a bright, bobbing light that could only be a calcium flare. A floating, chemically generated flare, usually attached to a lifebuoy, and a sure sign of trouble at sea!

Giffard's signalman directed his flashing light hopefully in the direction of the flare as Petersen headed his ship straight for it. There was now no question in his mind as to *Valleyfield*'s having met with some misfortune; either she had experienced an internal explosion, in her magazines or her boiler-room, perhaps, or she had been torpedoed or had struck a mine. But Petersen now made a fatal error; he failed to realize that the other ships in the group were ignorant of any mishap to their senior ship, and that he alone was aware of her disappearance.

As *Giffard* closed the scene of *Valleyfield*'s sinking, the remaining ships of the group continued on their course for St. John's; already they were miles away, out of sight in the hazy moonlight. Their radar operators, intent on detecting ice or other objects immediately in their path, failed to notice the disappearance of one of the line of contacts that represented the ships of their own group, stretched out on either beam, and, as the watches changed at midnight, nobody noticed the gap in the line.

Yet, all unwitting, the group was now favourably placed to intercept, detect, and destroy the U-boat that had torpedoed its leader. *U-548* was lying near the bottom, close on the port side; a square search pattern, if ordered now, would almost certainly have detected her, with HMCS *Halifax*, on the extreme left, particularly well placed. Fate was thrusting *Giffard*'s captain toward what seemed to be a hero's role; a signal to the group now, telling the other ships that *Valleyfield* had been sunk and ordering an "Observant" operation, or a square search, would almost certainly have turned up the U-boat, in conditions that should have given C-1 a kill. In the meantime, *Giffard*, now rapidly closing the scene of *Valleyfield*'s sinking, would have been able to pick up all of the frigate's survivors before the ice-cold water could have done them much harm. All that was needed to bring retribution to the U-boat, swift rescue to the survivors, and distinction for Petersen was a short signal to his group.

But what fate offered with one hand, it withdrew with the other; it left *Giffard*'s captain with a gnawing doubt, and doubt meant delay, and delay meant death for many of those struggling in the water and life for the U-boat that had put them there. The vital, urgent seconds ticked away, the ships of C-1 ploughed steadily northwards, away from their sinking leader and the lurking U-boat, while Petersen revolved the possibilities in his mind. What had happened to *Valleyfield*? An internal explosion? A mine? A torpedo? Until he was sure, he would make no signal, and he was still by no means sure.

As *Giffard* closed the scene of the sinking, the watchers on her bridge could make out wreckage floating in the water, then rafts loaded with men, and clusters of heads around them. Here and there was a solitary swimmer, clinging to a bit of flotsam; one of them had managed to switch on his survivor's light, a part of every service lifejacket but difficult for a swimmer to get at, and even more difficult to turn on and clip to the headdress, as the drill required.

The survivors, the amount of wreckage, and the pool of oil,

the stench of which could now clearly be made out, left no doubt as to *Valleyfield*'s having sunk, but what had caused the fatal disaster? If it were a mine or an internal explosion, Petersen could simply stop his ship in the midst of the wreckage and rescue all the survivors; it would be as simple as that. But if it were a U-boat that had torpedoed the frigate, *Giffard* would present an ideal target if she should stop, in this bright, calm sea, and lie wallowing for the half-hour or so required to take on board scores of oil-soaked, half-paralysed men. Torn by indecision, Petersen reduced speed and conned *Giffard* carefully into the midst of *Valleyfield*'s wreckage and survivors.

To the numbed *Valleyfield* crewmen, most of them now supported, in one way or another, by one of the Carley rafts or floater nets, the appearance of their consort brought a wave of emotion, a heady blend of relief and gratitude that brought a thin wave of cheering from the oil-slicked heads bobbing in little clusters in the icy water. Yeoman Kaplan, seated on a raft with a stunned seaman holding on to one leg, had seen *Giffard*'s light flashing a long way off moments before, as the corvette's signalman flashed his projector in a vain attempt to elicit a response from *Valleyfield*. Kaplan had yelled out, "There's a ship coming!" and everyone had stared hopefully at the signal light, which seemed high above the water. But the signalling had ceased and spirits had dropped momentarily, to be revived when *Giffard* herself appeared, her pastel paintwork bright in the misty moonlight, and seemed to tower far above the crowded survivors huddled on the surface.

The corvette slowed, almost to a stop, and came gliding up toward the nearest Carley float, awash under its overload of shivering men. And then it happened; loud and clear, its English accent magnified by the loud hailer, a voice boomed out: "HAVE YOU BEEN TORPEDOED?"

To the men in the water the question appeared so inane, so oblivious of the obvious desperation of their situation, that a hubbub of mingled incredulity and anger arose, above which could be heard the response of Lieutenant Warren, *Valleyfield*'s navigator:

"No, you stupid bastard, we just thought it seemed a nice night for a swim!"

A string of curses and imprecations followed as the exasperation and frustration of frightened men struggling for their very lives in the freezing water vented itself in raving fury. But despite their understandable rage, the question had not been the idle inanity it appeared; for Petersen, it was vital to establish whether or not there was an enemy U-boat lurking near by, and in amongst the shouted abuse he could make out the response that answered his question. *Valleyfield* had been torpedoed, and as his ship glided slowly through the frigate's scattered survivors he was deeply aware of what a perfect target she must now present to the nearby U-boat: almost stopped, broadside on to the moon, her camouflage paintwork making her a pale ghost on the mirror-like sea. Alone and vulnerable, he was too preoccupied to realize that his consorts were disappearing over the horizon, and that he had still to inform them of what had happened.

Technically, Petersen was not the senior officer of the remaining ships; Lieutenant-Commander R. D. "Rafe" Barrett, commanding officer of HMCS *Edmundston*, had seniority dating from exactly the same day as Petersen's, and as officers were grouped alphabetically under their seniority dates in the official Navy List, Barrett came before Petersen and therefore technically outranked him. But Petersen, displaying the firmness and initiative of a capable officer, realized that he was at the moment the only commanding officer aware of what had happened, and, as first on the scene and first to appreciate the situation, he took command and assumed the duties of senior officer of the stricken group. Until someone senior to him should appear on the scene and officially assume responsibility, Petersen would be in command of the operation. It was the age-old naval way, and as always it worked well, the transition from follower to leader being almost imperceptible, even to Petersen himself.

Giffard's commanding officer now found himself in an agony of indecision. There was a German U-boat close by; he knew from his asdic operator, who reported he had heard nothing, that the torpedo that had struck *Valleyfield* must have had a very short run, proving that the U-boat that had fired it had been at close range.

His first responsibility must be to seek out the U-boat and destroy it if he could; that was, after all, the whole purpose of his ship, what it had been designed for and what he and his crew were trained to do. Until he destroyed, or drove away, the lurking U-boat, no ship could stop in that flat, moonlit sea to pick up survivors without putting herself at fearful risk; risk of being herself torpedoed, and of adding her ship's company to the toll of dead and dying. Petersen fully realized the risk, and yet, and yet — nobody knew where the U-boat was. It might be miles away, and here, all about him, men were dying in the freezing water, men who were doomed unless he plucked them aboard — NOW!

In this fearful quandary, Petersen now did the human, understandable, but fallible thing: faced with two stark options, either of which could be disastrous, he attempted to compromise. He would not stop, and make a sitting duck of his ship, but he would not ignore the men in the water, either. He would slow down but not stop his ship, pick up what survivors he could, then proceed to hunt down the submarine. Accordingly, moving at dead slow, he steamed through the greatest concentration of survivors while his ship's company prepared to rescue as many men as possible.

Like all ocean escorts, *Giffard* carried scramble nets, made of strong manila line and attached inboard to her bulwarks along her waist, in the lowest part of the ship. These were now let down into the water on either side to assist men in the water to climb aboard, and husky seamen stood by to help pull survivors inboard, while other sailors coiled heaving lines ready to throw to nearby rafts and swimmers.

But although *Giffard* was moving very slowly, her momentum was far too great to allow any swimmer, let alone the numbed survivors from *Valleyfield*, already almost paralysed with cold, to grasp and hold on to the nets and lines now being offered them by the eager *Giffard* rescuers. The corvette's irresistible movement through the freezing water simply tore men from her side; no one could long hang on to, let alone scramble up, the sides of the moving ship. One Carley float managed to come along her port side, and the survivors aboard managed to catch a heaving line from *Giffard* and fasten it to their raft before it could be torn from their grasp.

As the raft drew in to the ship's side, the men crowded aboard it leaned outward to fend off and reach for a net or line. Their weight forced the forward part of their raft to dip further beneath the surface, and instantly it tipped and capsized under the forward pull of the moving ship, spilling its occupants into the water. Coder Munro hung grimly to the line he had grasped; out of the corner of his eye he could see the seaman who had been seated next to him looking up in mute horror as he was sucked astern under the corvette's counter and into the threshing propeller. Munro clung to his rope while eager hands reached for him, but rescue was impossible in the icy, irresistible current set up by the moving ship, and he was forced to let go and attempt to swim clear of *Giffard*'s stern. A few desperate strokes brought him to another raft, already laden with huddled figures, and Munro had just sufficient strength to haul himself painfully into it before he collapsed.

On his bridge, meanwhile, Petersen was painfully aware of his ship's vulnerability, crawling slowly across a moonlit sea in the presence of a known U-boat. Assistance, both to rescue survivors and to hunt the U-boat, was now vital, and accordingly he had finally made his signal to the remaining ships of his group: "CLOSE ME."

It was one minute past midnight, exactly twenty-three minutes after *Valleyfield* had been torpedoed.

Aboard *Halifax*, *Frontenac*, and *Edmundston*, *Giffard*'s signal arrived like a bombshell. It was just after the turn of the watch, and the new middle-watch keepers had not settled into their routine long enough to note the gap in the centre of their formation. *Frontenac*'s radar set was inoperable, and the new operators in the other ships were concentrating their attention ahead, for land or ice or other possible problems.

Irate commanding officers, awakened from their slumbers by alarmed officers of the watch, were angrily demanding answers which their dismayed juniors were unable to provide: Where was *Giffard*? Where was *Valleyfield*? Why wasn't Commander Byron giving orders, rather than Petersen? What in the blistering blue blazes had they been keeping station on, and would someone in this collection of crack-brained sleepwalkers kindly inform their concerned captain just what the hell was going on? Something along these general lines was now taking place on the bridge of each ship, and the agonized soul-searching was being vented in the expression of some pretty blunt home truths about the abilities of lookouts, radar operators, and, above all, officers of the watch.

Some of this inward turmoil inevitably found expression on the airwaves as baffled commanding officers consulted one another via inter-ship radio telephone. None of them had any idea of exactly where *Giffard* or *Valleyfield* was, and no inkling of what had happened. Petersen, far astern in *Giffard*, heard their consultations and, realizing this, made a further signal to them at eight minutes past midnight: ''VALLEYFIELD TORPEDOED.''

A full half-hour before, *Valleyfield* had been attacked and hit. In the intervening thirty minutes her riven hull had been convulsed by the spectacular agonies of her death throes before disappearing forever into the icy depths. Her officers and men, by the score, had died, swiftly or slowly, within her shattered hull and scores more were even now fighting for their very lives in the bone-freezing waste of oil-slicked water. All about, in bright moonlight, had been *Valleyfield*'s consorts, two ships on either side, equipped with the latest detection devices, manned by officers and men equipped with powerful binoculars, alert and watchful, and linked by every known means of communication, from light projectors to ultra-high-frequency radio. Yet ironically it was only now, half an hour later, that the ships of C-1 learned of the fate of their senior officer, his ship, and most of her men. Petersen's terse, two-word signal was the first intimation to anyone that *Valleyfield* had been torpedoed, an announcement loaded with implications.

Back at the scene of the sinking, Petersen had come to a decision. It was apparent that the unorganized attempts to rescue men while still maintaining steerage way would simply not suffice; if the freezing survivors were to be rescued, the ship would have to be stopped, and in the bright visibility conditions and in the known presence of a U-boat, the risk would be too great. His first responsibility must be to destroy or drive away the enemy submarine; accordingly Petersen increased speed and drew clear of the crowded survivors, taking *Giffard* back to the northwestward, streaming his CAT gear as he went as a precaution against acoustic torpedoes. *Giffard* had abandoned her role as rescuer and resumed her functions as a U-boat destroyer. While her consorts, now fully alerted and alarmed, felt their way back towards her, *Giffard* sallied forth to track down the hidden enemy.

Although Petersen could not know it, his quarry was not far away. Zimmermann had taken *U-548* clear to the northwestward at slow, silent speed, and was still within a few minutes' steaming. He had listened to *Frontenac*, *Halifax*, and *Edmundston* passing to the northward and, after an interval of silence, he heard the noise of *Giffard*'s quickened propeller beat and, loudest of all, the shrill scream of her CAT gear, which Zimmermann attributed to a "whistling buoy". He now stopped his engines and lay silent, a mere fathom or two above the ocean bed, awaiting developments. He was well within range of a determined surface hunt, and he knew it.

But up above, conditions were by no means as favourable for a hunt as they might have appeared. Such operations take time, as the target area is methodically searched, in carefully measured legs, to an established square pattern, and time was something *Giffard* could ill afford. From the beginning, her commander was preoccupied with anxiety for the men he had left struggling for their lives in the freezing water behind him. These endless, exasperating minutes dragging by while *Giffard* searched fruitlessly through an empty sea; was he squandering precious seconds, each one a man's life, in a vain search for an enemy now long gone?

The possibility of detecting the U-boat seemed more remote with each passing minute; as hope of establishing contact faded, the conviction grew that this sifting and searching of an empty sea was senseless. To Petersen, the U-boat was merely a presence, a wraith, never seen, now melted away into the remote depths from which it had come; the men, oil-soaked and half-paralysed with cold, were real and near, and they were dying, he knew, even as he searched vainly through this empty ocean for their vanished attacker.

The same sense of futility, of wasting precious moments looking for an enemy who was probably miles away, of conducting a pointless search for the proverbial needle in the haystack, pervaded *Giffard* at all levels. Officers and men alike shivered and stamped their feet and clapped their hands at their exposed action stations and wondered, sometimes audibly, what they were messing about here for when their mates were dying in the freezing water just astern of them. There was nothing to be seen, although they searched the misty horizon time and again; their radar screen showed no suspicious "blip", their asdic sent its transmissions into the depths on every side without receiving a single echo back. It was all a waste of precious time, surely.

Yet the effort had to be made, and *Giffard* duly made it. It was not a proper squared search that she made, and no "plot" or track chart was kept of it in her chart-room; she simply carried out a cursory and abbreviated sweep, by radar, asdic, and visual observation, of the immediate area to the northwestward of *Valleyfield*'s last known position. It was more of a gesture, a matter of carrying out the proper drill, than a serious attempt to hunt down a U-boat, and yet, surprisingly, it took *Giffard* almost within range of *U-548*. Listening intently on his hydrophones, his engines stopped, Zimmermann heard the "whistling buoy" coming towards him, heard the measured "ping" of *Giffard*'s asdic transmission searching the depths about him, before both became fainter as the corvette altered course to steer a new leg. If the search had been pressed home — but Petersen and his men had other things on their mind.

On the surface, a drastic and dramatic change had transformed the site of *Valleyfield*'s sinking. The spreading pool of oil, the burning calcium flare, the drifting rafts and floats were still there as before, but there was a marked change among the clustered survivors. For one thing, there were fewer of them; the fringes of men about each Carley float had thinned, as numbed hands lost their hold on the lifelines. There was little movement among the survivors; many of the swimmers floated motionless in their lifejackets, while the huddled figures sitting in the rafts slumped against one another in ominously frozen attitudes.

When *Giffard*, their only hope, had turned away from them, seemingly abandoning them to their fate, *Valleyfield*'s crewmen suffered a traumatic change of outlook. They had been so sure of rescue, so confident of surviving the sinking of their ship, that an attitude of expectancy had buoyed up their spirits and they had awaited their deliverance with a cheerful fortitude that made light of the freezing cold. But when *Giffard* had got under way, leaving them, as it seemed, to die, the heart went out of them. There was no singing now, no cheerful helping of one another to secure safer or more comfortable places on the rafts, only a glum silence. Suddenly the full realization of their situation was brought home to them; they were afloat in an icy sea, in a freezing cold that bit to the bone and was driving the life from their bodies. Every man was now aware that his life expectancy could be measured in minutes, and no rescuer in sight. The hardier, the more determined among them, clung desperately to life, strengthening their failing bodies with a desperate will to survive, but for many the challenge was too much for their failing strength. Abandoning themselves to the numbing depths reaching up for their bodies, they relinquished their handholds and slipped into the blissful surcease of unconsciousness.

In the dreadful minutes that followed *Giffard*'s departure, many young lives came to a merciful end. No despair now, no struggle, no agony; to *Valleyfield*'s freezing crewmen, Death came as a friend.

THE FIGHT FOR LIFE

IN THE DESPERATE struggle to survive that followed *Valleyfield*'s sinking, mind frequently triumphed over matter. The resolve to live, the determination not to yield, in many cases overcame the effects of choking oil and biting cold and enabled men to stay alive in conditions that proved fatal to many of their shipmates. Lieutenant Warren never lost heart, although he hovered on the brink of unconsciousness for long periods of time as he clung to anything that would help support him in a sea of congealing oil. Kaplan, the signal yeoman, was virtually invulnerable in his heavy zip-up zoot suit and spent much of his time assisting others less well clad to secure handholds on his overburdened raft. When he himself seemed in imminent danger of slipping off, he managed to clip himself to the lifeline by the steel clip shackle at the end of his lifejacket lanyard.

On the other side of the raft, Lieutenant Tate had also managed to clip himself to the lifeline of the Carley float. He had heard his captain, Lieutenant-Commander English, call out: "Count the men!" but, like Kaplan, he had been unable to make an accurate count of the piled-up heaps of oil-soaked bodies on the rafts and the vague clusters in the water surrounding them. He had called out to his captain, who, recognizing his voice, had said to him, in calm, low tones: "If I don't come out of this alive, Tate, call my wife."

"Aye aye, sir," Tate responded. "I will."

But as the long minutes dragged by, Tate himself began to slip into unconsciousness, only being jerked back to reality by some change in his circumstances. At first Lieutenant Reynolds was hanging on to the float on Tate's left, with Lieutenant Flath on his right, but after a time he noticed that both had slipped away during one of his blacked-out periods. Numbed by cold, both had drifted away unnoticed, and were never seen again.

It was noticeable now, as the oil layer thickened on the surface of the sea and gradually congealed with cold, that men with beards, of whom there were a considerable number, were experiencing difficulties. The heavy full beard, traditional in the service and proudly sported by officers and men alike, became matted with the tar-like floating bunker oil and became a serious hindrance as men sought to breathe through it, and to hold their faces clear of the water.

The burden of exhausted survivors on the three remaining Carley floats grew steadily heavier as individual swimmers made their way to them and clung for support. As the load increased, the raft life-rings were forced ever deeper in the water, and suddenly some of those whose lifejacket lanyards were clipped to the lifelines became aware that they were being dragged beneath the surface by the ever-sinking rafts. Most managed to unclip themselves in time, but Tate realized in sudden panic that he was unable to reach his clip and was in imminent danger of drowning as he was dragged ever lower.

Calling out in alarm, he attracted the attention of an able seaman sitting higher on the raft, René Baulne. Swiftly sizing up the situation, Baulne reacted with a speed surprising in one so numbed with cold. Quickly pulling out the knife that he carried, in traditional seaman's manner, in a sheath on his hip, Baulne reached over the huddled forms of heaped-up men and, grasping the submerged lanyard, cut it in two with a single stroke, undoubtedly saving Tate's life. It was one of many instances of the assistance that Baulne, from his central position, was able to give to the chilled fringe of survivors ringing the raft, or "his raft" as it seemed to be, since his personality engulfed and encouraged all who clung to it.

On a Carley float some distance away, Coder Ed Munro was experiencing quite a different situation. Half submerged on the raft, naked except for underwear shorts and his lifejacket, he felt the life being forced from his body by the biting cold of both sea and air. As his body grew numb, his mental processes slowed and he experienced periods of sleep-like blackout. Recovering from one of these, he noticed that the men clustered about him on the raft seemed surprisingly quiet and immobile, shrunken into their sodden clothing as if literally frozen into a shapeless huddle of miserable humanity, without voice or movement.

When a croaked question failed to awake any response from the man nearest him, Munro leaned forward and peered up into his face, shadowed by the monk-like hood of his duffle coat. The eyes were tight shut, the mouth gaped open; with a shock Munro realized that the man was dead. He looked round at the others, all leaning together, supporting one another in mutual misery. There was not the slightest response to his hoarse inquiry, not the least facial tremor, not a single glint of recognition in any of the eyes staring blankly from oil-smudged faces. With a sudden clutch of fear at his heart, Munro realized that they were all dead, killed by cold and wet and shock in the clump they had made as they huddled together in a desperate attempt to preserve their last vestiges of warmth.

It was the stuff of nightmares; as he drifted off into welcome unconsciousness, Munro knew that he was adrift with a crew of dead men, the only living soul on this raft of death. From this nightmare world of reality he escaped gratefully into the dream world of oblivion, and knew no more of ship sinkings, of suffering and death.

Endless as this ordeal seemed to *Valleyfield*'s suffering wretches on rafts and in the water, it lasted little more than an hour. Aboard the corvette *Giffard*, Petersen had given over his cursory radar and sonar search as soon as the returning ships of C-1 hove into sight. Ordering them to carry out Operation Observant, a systematic square search of ever-increasing proportions centred on the site of *Valleyfield*'s sinking, Petersen turned his own ship about and hastened back toward the little huddle of survivors, who had been on his mind throughout, a concern that had drastically limited his search for the U-boat.

In a few minutes of fast steaming he brought the survivors in sight again, and with the search for the enemy now in the hands of others, he devoted his full attention to rescuing the frigate's crewmen as swiftly and efficiently as possible. He brought *Giffard* gently into the midst of the rafts and wreckage, being careful to keep her headed directly into the moon so as to present the smallest silhouette possible to any U-boat commander seeking an easy target, before taking most of the way off her, without bringing her to a complete stop.

Eager crewmen lined the waist of the corvette and began to pull *Valleyfield*'s exhausted men over the low side. Many survivors were so numbed and weary that they were incapable of any effort, beyond clutching at the lines thrown them; they had to be assisted, or literally carried inboard, by *Giffard*'s rescuers, who went overside down the scramble nets to grip them and boost them up and over.

At the same time as this rescue work was going on, *Giffard* launched her sea-boat, the short, sturdy little pulling boat carried by all corvettes, and *Edmundston* sent her sea-boat too, under the command of Lieutenant David Kerr, to range around the outer fringes of the scene, rescuing individual survivors, either swimming alone or clinging to wreckage, who had been unable to make their way to the crowded Carley floats.

The first of such survivors encountered was Lieutenant Warren, the frigate's navigator, who was hauled unceremoniously aboard and lay gasping in the bottom of *Edmundston*'s boat, numbed and exhausted and oil-sodden and near the limit of his endurance.

But the work of rescue proved dangerous to rescuer and rescued alike. *Valleyfield*'s captain, who had managed to survive, without a lifejacket, all the perils and hardships of this dreadful night, reached *Giffard*'s side from his handhold on a Carley float. But he was virtually at the end of his tether; grasping at the scramble net over the corvette's side, he attempted to pull himself from the water, against the pull of the ship, still under way, but his strength was not equal to the effort. Willing hands reached to him from the corvette's rail, but he was unable to grasp them. Seeing his plight, one of *Giffard*'s crewmen seized him by the back of his uniform tunic and attempted to lift him upward. With a lifejacket, the effort would have been successful, but the light material of the uniform was inadequate to the demands being made upon it. Buttons parted, seams ripped, as the whole weight of the captain's body was taken by the soaked fabric; with a splash, English slipped from the sleeves of his jacket and fell back overside. The last seen of this gallant officer, whose careful attention to the wearing of lifejackets had saved the lives of so many of his men but not his own, was of his upturned face as he disappeared into the oily depths alongside.

Like their captain, some of *Valleyfield*'s exhausted crewmen survived the hardships of the sinking, only to fall victim to the difficulties and dangers of getting aboard *Giffard* at the very moment of rescue. Some men were unconscious, and the task of getting their heavy bodies, sodden with water and slippery with oil, up and over the steep steel sides of the corvette, as she moved slowly, but remorselessly, ahead was sometimes more than the strength of their shipmates and their hard-pressed rescuers could manage. The biting cold numbed mental as well as physical faculties, making men incapable of recognizing the difficulties of a situation, let alone coming up with a solution.

Some sat unmoving, staring with uncomprehending eyes at the waving hands of would-be rescuers while they floated serenely past to the certain death that waited astern. Others, and they were the majority, simply lacked the strength to catch a line or hold on to a net and were totally dependent for their rescue on the efforts of the hard-working handful of men who were all that could find space along *Giffard*'s side and scramble nets. Some few were accordingly lost, but the corvette's crew managed to save nearly all, hauling them up, soaked and slimy, by the brute strength of arms near cracking from fatigue and overwork.

Lieutenant Tate was hauled up, not in the crowded corvette waist, but from the towering height of *Giffard*'s fo'c'sle, catching hold of a bight of canvas fire-hose dangled down to him from there by Lieutenant Patterson, *Giffard*'s first lieutenant, and other eager rescuers. Tate managed to get the hose slipped around and under him, and was hauled bodily up the side with no further effort on his part.

For Kaplan, the signal yeoman, the rescue proved nearly fatal.

In better shape than most of his comrades in the water because of the full-length heavy water-resistant suit he was wearing, he had spent nearly all the long minutes on his life raft supporting one or more of his less well-clad shipmates. Arriving alongside *Giffard*, he had passed the support of an unconscious seaman to a rescuer leaning from above, only to find that he himself was unable to move. His lifejacket lanyard was still clipped to the lifeline of the Carley float, not only holding him fast but dragging him down to the surface as the raft sank ever lower with the surge of weight to the side nearest the corvette.

"Somebody give me a dirk!" he shouted, calling for the sheath knife many seamen carried, and then, as the raft sank even lower and he scrabbled desperately for the unreachable clip, "Give me a dirk! Give me a dirk!"

One of *Giffard*'s seamen drew his knife and it was hurriedly passed down to Kaplan. A slash, a struggle, another slash, and he was free; half fainting with relief, he clambered inboard to safety.

A macabre situation developed when the corvette eased alongside the raft carrying Coder Munro and his dead shipmates. Munro himself was now totally unconscious and seemingly lifeless when the raft was caught with a boathook and pulled alongside. The first two bodies hauled, with immense difficulty, up to the corvette's deck were obviously dead, and were moved out of the way and left to one side until further attention could be paid to them. Munro's motionless form was also heaved up painfully, inch by excruciating inch, and his frozen body was dumped beside the other two. But with live men calling for rescue and clutching desperately at *Giffard*'s side, the corvette's hard-pressed crew had no time or effort to waste on dead men, and a quick check of those remaining on the raft showed that all life was extinct. The raft was accordingly bundled aside to make way for those whose lives might yet be saved, and the desperate battle for rescue was resumed.

One by one, as they were hauled inboard, the choking, gasping, half-frozen *Valleyfield* men were hustled forward into the waiting messdecks, to be hurriedly towelled, wrapped in blankets, and put to bed on the cushioned locker tops that ringed each mess. Warmth was the goal: warm drinks were poured down chilled throats, icy limbs were chafed and wrapped in warm wool, warm messdecks made a cosy refuge from the freezing night air and chilling water. The injured men — and there were a good few — received treatment for their hurts from *Giffard*'s sick-berth attendant, Howard Bailey, while the corvette's coxswain and first lieutenant were everywhere, organizing and directing their ship's every resource to rescue, restore, and comfort their comrades from the stricken frigate.

Yet as always in the chancy conditions of a rescue at sea, luck — or fate — played a part, too. Temporarily left for dead on the exposed upper deck, Ed Munro was, in fact, very near death, but still alive. He would undoubtedly have died in the few minutes before he could have been examined more thoroughly had not a passing engine-room artificer, on his way past the pile of supposedly dead bodies in the waist, happened to notice a slight movement of a bare leg in their midst.

"This one's alive! Give us a hand!" he shouted, and in a moment willing arms had gathered up the supposed corpse and carried it into the light and warmth of the messdecks. Warm drinks, a vigorous towelling, and a wrap-up in a warm blanket soon brought results and Munro opened his eyes to find himself, not in the icy sea he had last seen before he slipped into unconsciousness, but in the warm messdecks of *Giffard*, with anxious faces peering down at him. For the near-naked coder it was, quite literally, a return from the dead.

On the bridge, an anxious Petersen paced back and forth while the agonizing, time-consuming task of rescue went on. For all that he was careful to keep *Giffard* headed directly into the moon's path, presenting the smallest silhouette possible, his ship was a prime target, lying almost stopped on a smooth, moonlit sea, and he knew it. But he was resolved to remain until every last survivor had been rescued and he kept his ship there, with engines slowly turning over, until the last Carley float had been retrieved, the last bit of wreckage examined, the waters searched for any lone swimmers who had not already been picked up by the two corvettes' sea-boats.

Eventually the boats returned, their search completed, and were left adrift after disgorging their rescued and their rescuers. When at last he had satisfied himself that the work was complete, Petersen got his ship about, cranked up revolutions for full speed, and resumed course for St. John's. Speed was of the essence, for he realized that there were men on board whose lives might well depend upon reaching hospital with the shortest possible delay. Laden with her burden of men suffering from hypothermia, from shock and exposure, *Giffard* departed from the scene, her part in the double tragedy complete.

She left behind her the remaining ships of C-1, now restored to an efficient operating team under the direction of Lieutenant-Commander Barrett in the corvette *Edmundston*. The last vestige of Channel Fever had long since disappeared; it was not making port that concerned the remaining officers and men of the group, but rather exacting revenge for the sinking of their leader. Spread in line abreast they carried out the methodical sweep of Operation Observant, searching beneath the sea with their probing asdics for any trace of the U-boat they knew could not be far away.

They were not disposed to be choosy; any echo, however faint, any contact, however fleeting, was attacked. *Edmundston* fired a hedgehog pattern at an elusive, will-o'-the-wisp contact which proved abortive; the charges detonated harmlessly on the bottom and the echo, probably a temperature anomaly, faded into nothingness. Shortly after 1 a.m., just an hour and a half after *Valleyfield* had been torpedoed, the first depth-charges rained down on a suspicious contact.

It was not *U-548*, however; Zimmermann had taken her clear of the initial leg of the surface search, and heard the rumble and bang of the charges exploding well out of range. He decided to lie still and silent, and accordingly took the U-boat even deeper, until she gently came to rest on the sea bottom.

As the legs of the surface search widened, the ships of C-1 came ever closer, but Zimmermann's nerve never failed; an hour later two of the ships passed directly over him, their CAT gear screaming like banshees in his hydrophones, but Zimmermann's confidence in the security of his nest on the sea bottom was justified. No asdic contact was made, no depth-charges were dropped, and as the ships faded into the distance Zimmermann judged it was a prudent time to move on. Running at dead slow, he lifted off the bottom and steered quietly away to the southwest. And so, at about 4 a.m., another principal player, the villain of the piece, slunk from the stage, to the accompaniment, hours later, of two depth-charge attacks, made by aircraft. Zimmermann now headed for a patrol area off Halifax, where he hoped for less dangerous quarry.

In St. John's, naval authorities reacted swiftly to the news of *Valleyfield*'s sinking, reported to them in a signal from *Giffard*.

The frigate *New Glasgow* was sent with all dispatch to the scene, along with the corvettes *Timmins* and *Agassiz* of Escort Group W-2, the two ships that had been passed earlier by *Valleyfield* as they proceeded outwards to search for a suspected U-boat. As *Giffard* headed for St. John's, these three new ships joined with the three ships of C-1 — *Frontenac*, *Halifax*, and *Edmundston*, under the command of the latter — in a really intensive search for the responsible U-boat.

As these fresh ships joined, Barrett in *Edmundston* altered and broadened the sweep from the merely local hunt of Operation Observant into a much larger organized search — Operation Salmon — designed to cast its net still further. All through the next day the hunt went on, the six ships intensively combing out an area of many square miles in ever-widening legs. On one of these slow, deliberate sweeps, *Edmundston* was rewarded with an echo that for the first time sounded promising: a firm, hard reflection from a target, seemingly of the right size, lying stationary on the sea bed. It could well be the U-boat, lying doggo, hoping to escape notice while the hunters swept over her, so with hopes high, *Edmundston* went in for a deliberate attack.

The charges, delivered with precision on the carefully stalked target, rained down, there was a tremendous explosion as they went off in the relatively shallow depths, and eager eyes scanned the surface as the fountains of spray from the attack subsided. And there, there! There was something coming up from the bottom!

While her crewmen craned eagerly to see what their attack had brought up, *Edmundston* cruised slowly through the disturbed water and floating debris of her attack. A widening pool of oil, a spreading slick that quickly covered a wide area, raised hopes still further, and the watchers focussed attention on a dark, chunky object that bobbed to the surface in the midst of the oil. There was something horribly familiar about its outline, about the lettering on its back —

It was a Canadian naval lifejacket. There could be no mistaking that distinctive design, or its uniquely Canadian origin; no other lifejacket, mercantile or naval service, was remotely like it. And with the recognition of its origin came another, darker realization: it could only have come from *Valleyfield*. They had been attacking the shattered wreck of their group leader, disturbing the steel tomb where so many of their comrades lay forever entrapped.

Sick at heart, the men of *Edmundston* resumed the hunt for the elusive U-boat, but hope of gaining contact was now fading fast; with each passing hour the area of possible search increased to impossible proportions. At nightfall of the third day, seventy hours after the sinking, the hopeless search was abandoned, and the six ships trailed disconsolately back to harbour.

Far to the south, their elusive quarry was trundling along in thick fog, running submerged with only occasional visits to the surface to charge his batteries. Zimmermann had acted on his own initiative in changing *U-548*'s patrol area, and was relieved to learn, some twenty-two hours after he had made the decision to shift operations to the Halifax area, that his superiors in Germany had arrived at similar conclusions. A terse wireless message from Operations, addressed to Zimmermann, noted that if conditions were unfavourable, he should shift operations further south. By the time this message was received, Zimmermann had already done so and was approaching his new patrol area.

While the fruitless hunt for *U-548* was going on, *Giffard* was proceeding, at her best speed, for St. John's, her messdecks jammed with exhausted, chilled, and oil-soaked men. Some were dead, others dying, many of them ill or injured. Some lay in trance-like comas, others retched agonizingly as they brought up the oil and saltwater mixture that was poisoning them. *Giffard*'s crewmen did what they could for their suffering comrades, not only in helping their hard-pressed medical team minister to the injured, but in giving up anything they possessed — blankets, clothing, hammocks, cigarettes — that could help or comfort the survivors from their sister ship. Howard Bailey, *Giffard*'s sick-berth attendant, worked untiringly among the ill or injured, administering pain-killers, cleaning and bandaging wounds. As *Giffard* raced through the night, her company fought to cherish and sustain the lives of their fellow seamen with all the sea's traditional sacrifice and selflessness.

Survivors

Of all *Valleyfield*'s ice-numbed, oil-soaked survivors, perhaps none was in as good condition as Irving Kaplan, her yeoman of signals. Once he had unzippered his cocoon-like zoot suit and towelled himself warm and dry, Kaplan quickly recovered from the effects of his ordeal and, clothed in borrowed sweater, trousers, and boots, was the first of the shattered frigate's crew able to take stock of the situation. Anxious to see which of his shipmates had survived, and to check on their condition, he began to circulate among the huddled groups of seamen, most of them barely conscious, in *Giffard*'s crowded messdecks and cabin flats.

There were quite a few familiar faces, he noted, all obviously suffering from shock, and at least two officers — Lieutenant Tate in the forward messdeck and Lieutenant Warren in one of the cabins — but nowhere could he find his captain. It was only now that the full scale of the disaster began to be realized; out of *Valleyfield*'s complement of more than one hundred and sixty officers and men, only a small portion were assembled here on the decks of the little corvette.

In the course of his rounds, Kaplan encountered *Giffard*'s coxswain, who had set out to count heads, and between them they went round to establish the exact numbers of living and dead from *Valleyfield* now on board. Kaplan's first count was thirty-nine, but on comparing notes with the coxswain he realized that he had duplicated a couple of names; there were, the two agreed, exactly five dead and thirty-eight living on board from the torpedoed frigate. Only two of her fifteen officers and thirty-six of her one hundred and forty-eight crewmen had survived the disaster.

It was a shocked and weary Kaplan who crawled into a vacant hammock in the early hours of the morning and sought the surcease of sleep as *Giffard* raced through the night towards the distant amenities of St. John's, and the aid and comfort which only the shore could provide.

The strident clamour of the alarm bells ringing "action stations", and the resultant tumult as *Giffard*'s sleeping seamen tumbled out on deck, roused Kaplan a few hours later. A glance at his watch showed that it was only 0530, and the call proved to be a false alarm; a suspicious radar contact proved to be, not a surfaced U-boat but merely an isolated "growler" or small iceberg, but as the corvette crewmen returned to their interrupted slumbers, Kaplan found himself too restless to sleep, and set out instead to make the rounds of his shipmates, most of them now awake and fearful.

Lieutenant Tate, in fact, had already recovered sufficiently to move around a bit, and after circulating about the messdecks had put his head into the cabin where Lieutenant Warren lay exhausted. Aware of his presence, Warren opened his eyes and, recognizing his visitor, managed a broad, slow wink.

"Hi-ho, Tater!" he whispered.

"Hi-ho, Jaker!" Tate responded, and left him to his slumbers.

Tate himself, in fact, was weaker than he had realized and in a minute or two, virtually dead on his feet, he returned gratefully to his blankets in *Giffard*'s warm messdeck, where a few minutes later Kaplan found him. Conversing in whispers, so as not to disturb the sleepers all about them, Tate suggested that Kaplan, as the most active of the survivors, should take the details of each survivor's story and write them down, so that they would be preserved, while still fresh, for the official inquiries that lay ahead.

Accordingly, having secured pencil and paper, Kaplan began to circulate among those of *Valleyfield*'s men who were awake and in fit condition to talk, and so, bit by painful bit, the individual stories of the frigate's sinking began to emerge, stories that would continue to be told, in increasing detail and with inevitable distortion as memory faded, for years to come.

Armed with this scribbled journal, Kaplan returned to Warren's cabin and found him much restored and able to talk. He dictated to the yeoman his own recollection of events before and after the sinking, and after Kaplan had finished recording them the pair set out, accompanied by *Giffard*'s coxswain, to officially identify the bodies of *Valleyfield*'s dead, huddled together under cover on the corvette's quarterdeck: Lieutenant Reynolds; Petty Officer Hoffman; Shipwright Therrien; Bill Burton, the Supply Assistant; and Archie Mills, a coder.

It was a relief to return from the dead to the living; the little party returned gratefully to the warm messdecks, where the survivors, most of them by now revived and restored, were taking stock of their situation, while René Baulne, their guardian angel, fussed about them, as indeed he had for most of the night.

Baulne, alone among *Valleyfield*'s seamen, seemed almost untouched by the harrowing events of the frigate's sinking and the long ordeal of her survivors in the freezing cold of the North Atlantic. He had managed to keep himself free of the worst of the fuel oil that had encumbered so many of his shipmates, and had withstood the biting cold that had numbed the minds and ravaged the bodies of most of his fellow survivors. Mentally and physically he had come through the frightful events of the night in better shape than almost anyone, and had emerged as both a leader and an inspirer of men.

It was he who had saved Lieutenant Tate's life by cutting him free from the sinking life raft, and who had helped cherish his raft-load of shaken survivors through their night-long ordeal. Once hauled aboard *Giffard*, he had been the first to recover from the effects of the sinking, and had spent the rest of the night hours in helping with the cleaning and care of his shipmates.

It was he who had accompanied Kaplan on his rounds, and who had worked with *Giffard*'s coxswain in ensuring that all the survivors were warm and as comfortable as was humanly possible. As *Giffard* neared the approaches to St. John's, Baulne was able to look back with some satisfaction on the part he had played in the survival of the little knots of shipmates huddled in blankets all about him.

The growing light of morning, and the sudden activity of the new day as *Giffard*'s crewmen, roused from their slumbers by the shrilling of a bosun's pipe and the cheerful slap on their hammock bottom of a passing bosun's mate, began the unvarying routine of a ship's day. There were hammocks to lash and stow, breakfast to be brought from the galley, scores of hungry men to feed, and dozens of guests in their midst to be made welcome, to laugh and joke with, to be comforted or exclaimed over.

The activity reached a new pitch as the breakfast dishes were cleared away and a new watch prepared to close up to stations, to be replaced by dozens of chilled off-watch seamen and weary stokers, all hungry for their breakfasts. *Giffard* would soon be entering harbour, and as the ship rolled on towards Cape Spear and the turn into the narrows, her crew was fully occupied in making the ship and themselves presentable, the organized chaos of washing and shaving, cleaning and polishing, that inevitably accompanies a naval vessel's return to port.

For the first time since their arrival onboard, *Valleyfield*'s survivors, those who were well enough, found themselves with breathing space, alone amidst the busy tumult all about them, and able to take stock of their situation.

For most, it was the first occasion when the full import of what had happened to them was brought home to them. They were alive, and would go on living. They were a chosen few. Back there, in the icy depths they themselves had left mere hours before, lay their shipmates, the friends and companions of yesterday now made remote and strangely distant by the mystery of death.

Fate had been at work; in those crowded minutes in the icy moonlight, it had taken this man, spared that one. It had taken, indeed, most of their shipmates, for as they glanced about them in the growing light, the realization of how few remained was borne crushingly home to the huddled groups in the alien messdecks. They sucked their cigarettes and glanced wide-eyed about them, the exultation of survival now sobered by their growing awareness of the magnitude of the disaster that had engulfed them, of the fearful numbers of faces they would never see again.

But time for reflection was brief; the busy, intrusive world of the living allowed little scope for morbid thoughts. Early in the afternoon, there was the bosun's pipe shrilling through the ship: "Hands to stations for entering harbour! Special sea-duty men close up!"

Bearing her burden of living and dead, the saved and the saviours, His Majesty's Canadian Ship *Giffard* ran her clean harbour ensign up to the gaff and her pennant numbers to the yard-arm, and made her turn in to the narrow gut that led into St. John's under the frowning cliffs of Signal Hill. For her officers on the bridge, for her fresh-scrubbed seamen fallen into ordered ranks on fo'c'sle head and quarterdeck, the long ordeal of the night before was ending. For her captain, pale and hollow-cheeked from lack of sleep, now conning his ship in past Chain Rock, the nightmare was only beginning.

The officers and men of HMCS *Avalon*, the navy's sprawling shore base in St. John's, had been astir for hours. *Giffard*'s signal reporting the loss of the frigate *Valleyfield* had set off a mounting wave of activity. Junior watch-keepers in operational rooms had consulted their seniors, who, in turn, signals in hand, had awakened their commanding officers and, ultimately, the handful of very senior officers who directed every field of operations in St. John's, the farthest-flung of the Royal Canadian Navy's operational bases.

There were innumerable things to be done, and to be done at once, if not sooner. Ships were to be dispatched, ships now lying, darkened and asleep, at the crowded South Side jetties across the harbour from the city, where the frigates and corvettes of the escort groups were berthed three and four deep. Air force authorities had to be notified, aircraft made ready and their crews awakened and briefed for the patrols that must be flown over the disaster area. Signals had to be dispatched, to escort groups at sea, to the operations room in far-off Derby House in Liverpool, where the Commander in Chief, Western Approaches, ran the unremitting war on U-boats in every part of the Atlantic, and to Naval Service Headquarters in Ottawa, where the news would waken the nation's most senior naval officers from their slumbers in consternation and alarm.

But, above all, it was in the naval hospital on the hill above the old port city that the signal had the most immediate, the most pressing, effect. For *Giffard*'s signal had indicated that there were survivors, and survivors was what the hospital was set up for. Nowhere on this side of the Atlantic was there a medical facility with more experience of survivors, those shivering, sodden, oil-soaked wretches, half drowned, fearfully burned or mangled, plucked from torpedoed merchantmen, burning tankers, rammed escorts, or crashed aircraft, and brought, often more dead than alive, to the huddle of wartime emergency buildings that comprised the RCN hospital in St. John's. Here, in this easternmost Atlantic outpost, the medical science of a sophisticated urban civilization came to grips with the raw realities of a world at war. Here, if anywhere, were the skilled, experienced men and women capable of reviving, nurturing, and restoring the faintest flicker of life in men snatched from fiery wrecks or freezing seas.

The young — the hospital's Senior Medical Officer was traditionally only a surgeon commander — medical officers and nursing sisters who operated the hospital, for all their experience, were relatively new to the naval service, but they included some of the brightest and ablest of the new crop of nurses, physicians, and surgeons from hospitals and schools of medicine across Canada, seasoned by some of the most notable names in private medical practice. All had been hand-picked for posting to this base, in the forefront of the Battle of the Atlantic, and their mettle was now to be thoroughly tested.

Giffard's signal had set preparations in motion as surgeons were shaken awake, nurses and orderlies roused, wards and operating rooms got ready. A fleet of ambulances was dispatched to await *Giffard* at her allotted berth, and it was these vehicles, drawn up in an orderly rank, that greeted the corvette's crewmen as *Giffard* came slowly alongside.

The moment her lines were secured, the urgent business of transferring the survivors ashore was put in motion, most of them borne by stretcher to the waiting ambulances, but a few of the best-recovered seamen making their own way ashore and taking their places for the short ride up to the hospital on the hill. On this emergency occasion *Giffard* was allowed to berth alongside a pier on the north side of the harbour, the ''city side'', rather than at the usual corvette tiers that stretched along the South Side, thus sparing her suffering passengers the long, jolting ride around the harbour.

The two officer survivors, by now feeling fairly perky, were able to take an interest in their surroundings and were beginning to savour their status as celebrities. Seeing a naval staff car parked alongside, Lieutenant Warren headed for it and, with Lieutenant Tate sitting beside him, bade the driver to head for the hospital and the pair drove off in style.

On arrival, they were directed to their waiting beds in the officers' ward by an astonished nurse, but they stopped at a bathroom along the corridor to clean themselves up. A row of gleaming white shower stalls beckoned, irresistible to men still smeared with fuel oil beneath their grubby clothing; within seconds they were luxuriating in the steamy blessings of hot showers, washing away the stink and scum of the all-pervasive oil which had been a part of the nightmare ordeal ever since *Valleyfield* had been torpedoed.

They were reluctantly torn from the showers by a horrified

orderly, to be further scolded by an even more seriously concerned doctor. They had, they were told, just done the worst possible thing for patients suffering from prolonged exposure to severe cold; too rapid heating of the body could lead to all sorts of nasty reactions, particularly in the body's extremities, where gangrene, and the resultant need for amputation, was always a threat. They were hustled into bed, along with the remainder of their shipmates, who had now arrived by the more conventional ambulance route, and a course of treatment was begun.

They were fortunate to be under the care of two exceptional medical officers, Surgeon Lieutenant A. L. Johnson, an enterprising young man working under the direction of Surgeon Captain Charles Best, who, in civilian life, had teamed with Dr. Banting in the exhaustive experiments that led to the development of insulin as a treatment for diabetes, and who had been flown in especially to help treat *Valleyfield*'s survivors. This two-man medical team now instituted a novel method of treatment. Their patients were propped up in bed so that their feet and hands were exposed to a current of air, blown by electric fans suitably arranged over pans of ice cubes, the chill airstream thus ensuring that the body extremities did not warm up too quickly and thus bring on gangrene.

This unusual arrangement was entirely successful; despite their prolonged exposure to the biting temperatures of both air and sea, *Valleyfield*'s survivors all made full and complete recoveries, the only casualty being one seaman's little toe, which had to be amputated.

As they recovered, the survivors were sent off home on long leave; the early birds, those least affected and thus quickest to recover, went off individually, the remainder in a jubilant body.

For Lieutenants Warren and Tate, the ten-day stay in hospital was a pleasant time. Like their shipmates, they enjoyed being the centre of attention of reporters and photographers and attentive nurses. An attractive physiotherapist, Stella Davidson, who prescribed exercises to restore muscle and body tone for the survivors, in particular caught the eye of Lieutenant Tate, and they were soon fast friends.

But there was a sombre note underlying the general air of relief at having survived; the euphoria of being alive was underlined by the consciousness of the great majority of *Valleyfield* shipmates who had died in the common catastrophe. This tragic aspect was brought home with sobering emphasis soon after *Giffard*'s arrival in port, when the funeral was held for the five dead she had brought in with the living: Lieutenant Frank C. Reynolds, Ordnance Artificer Martin J. Hoffman, Coder Archie W. Mills, Supply Assistant William C. Burton, and Shipwright Joseph C. Therrien.

It was a major ceremonial event, with all the measured pomp and circumstance of full naval honours. More than a thousand men, drawn from the naval establishment in St. John's, including contingents from the ships in harbour as well as naval ratings from barracks and shore establishments, marched in ordered procession to the stately measure of the funeral march. Behind the naval band, the long parade wound its way out along Water Street, past the park, to the old cemetery on the hills behind the city and there, among the graves of the dead from ancient wars, the sailors laid the bodies of their young shipmates slain in this new conflict. The sea breeze ruffled the hair of hundreds of bowed bare heads, the bugles and the traditional three volleys of the firing party echoed from the barren hills, and the lovely language of the naval prayer and the pure beauty of the white naval ensigns wrought their magic. On this rocky hilltop thrust into the Atlantic wastes, Canada mourned its naval dead with all the moving pageantry inherited from that mother of all the world's fleets, Britain's Royal Navy.

With the tending of the living and the burial of the dead, the immediate results of the catastrophe had all been dealt with, and with the return to harbour of the surface forces, under the direction of the new C-1 acting senior officer in *Edmundston*, after a long and fruitless hunt, the emergency precipitated by *Valleyfield*'s torpedoing had come to an end. Now the naval establishment turned its attention to the cause of the disaster, to the assessing of blame and credit, and to a full examination of the circumstances of the sinking to determine what lessons, if any, could profitably be learned. As with all instances of naval loss, a court of inquiry must be held.

Court of Inquiry

A FORMAL COURT of inquiry into the sinking of HMCS *Valleyfield* was held in St. John's on May 10, 1944, with Captain S. W. Davis, RCN, as president and Lieutenant-Commander F. O. Gerity, RNCR, and Lieutenant-Commander W. G. Ross, RCNVR, as members. Its object was: "To inquire into the loss of HMCS *Valleyfield*, and the death and injuries of certain officers and ratings on board the said ship at the time". But once the investigation began, it became evident that the board must concern itself with two separate and distinct aspects, both of which were tragedies involving considerable loss of life: the torpedoing, while steaming in company, of *Valleyfield*, and the subsequent conduct of rescue operations by the group. Because the most senior officers concerned were now dead, the first part tended to be something of an academic exercise; it was the second part, involving the responsibilities and the conduct of officers living and present, that inevitably dominated proceedings.

The board heard evidence from a wide range of officers and men in the various ships involved, much of it inconclusive and some of it conflicting in minor details, before finding that *Valleyfield* had been sunk by a torpedo fired by a submarine, down moon, on the frigate's port bow. Beyond that, and some remarks as to the inadequacy of existing lifesaving equipment, the board had little to say, but its silence on certain aspects of the proceedings after the frigate's sinking was significant.

It remained for the two most senior officers at St. John's, Commodore Cuthbert Taylor, RCN, Flag Officer, Newfoundland, and Captain James Rowland, DSC, RN, Captain (D), to make the most pertinent comment on the group's conduct in a series of remarks appended to the court report.

In addition to the accounts of individual survivors then in hospital, the board had as evidence statements from the commanding officer of HMCS *Edmundston*, together with those of her first lieutenant and the officer of the watch at the time of the sinking, and the full report of proceedings by the commanding officer of *Giffard*, in addition to all the supporting data as to the operational situation at the time of the disaster.

There was a moment of light relief during the board's preliminary inquiries when evidence had to be taken from Lieutenants Tate and Warren in hospital. A white naval ensign was spread over the counterpane of Warren's bed to provide a suitable touch of service decorum to the proceedings while the pair, propped up on pillows, recalled for the benefit of the officers lounging about their room the happenings of that memorable night, while a secretary at bedside recorded the proceedings in shorthand.

The account that emerged from the mass of evidence about the initial part of the disaster, the torpedoing, was all too clearly utterly damning. An anti-submarine group, without any convoy or other burdening responsibilities, and in excellent asdic operating conditions, steaming without zigzag at steady course and speed and without CAT gear streamed through mirror-calm seas in bright moonlight ideal for torpedo attack, had had its senior ship torpedoed and sunk by the very enemy submarine it had been warned to expect, and in the very area it had been warned to expect it. To any investigating body viewing the unquestioned facts in the cold light of day, the circumstances of the torpedoing seemed a devastating indictment of the senior officer of the group, Commander J. Byron, DSC, RN, the officer responsible for the disposition and procedures of Escort Group C-1. He had failed to detect the approach of a U-boat about which he had been specifically warned, he had steamed through the area where he had been warned it was operating without any concession of course or speed to make his group a less attractive target, and, despite the terrible lessons learned by escorts in recent months, he had failed to take any precautions against the new, and deadliest, U-boat weapon, the acoustic torpedo. It was a woeful chronicle of failure, an invitation to disaster, viewed from the calm serenity of the boardroom by Commodore Taylor and Captain Rowland.

But these officers were men of experience of operations at sea; men who understood the infinite number of factors that had always to be borne in mind by the captains of ships under way. No decision at sea could be presented as a simple choice between black and white, right and wrong; rather, it involved choosing between a variety of courses, all coloured in varying shades of grey. Both officers could appreciate Commander Byron's decision to cancel the initial zigzag, an anti-torpedo course steered by the group, in the face of the mounting danger presented by low-lying ice, too low to be detected by radar but heavy enough to crush the light steel hull of any of his ships. In his view, the ice presented the greater danger; it *was* present, whereas the U-boat might well not be.

So far as the signalled warning of the U-boat's presence was concerned, all ships had become accustomed to such signals on an almost daily basis, but in very few instances was the U-boat ever seen or detected. The sea is vast, and the chances of contact with a suspected submarine in the enormous empty expanses of ocean were always remote.

The decision not to stream CAT gear was also understandable. The gear conferred security from acoustic-torpedo attack, but at the cost of almost all asdic operating efficiency, the tremendous noise from astern virtually drowning out all but the clearest of echoes from any quarter. Byron's decision not to stream CAT gear until in the presence of a detected U-boat was easily appreciated by any officer of experience; after all, C-1 represented, not a vulnerable huddle of merchantmen, but a group of warships specifically designed and trained to detect and destroy submarines. In any encounter with a U-boat, they would naturally assume the role of the hunter, rather than the hunted, and therefore their prime concern was the efficiency of their hunting equipment, rather than their own safety. Warships, as Sir John Fisher had noted, were built to be sunk.

Viewed from the point of view of an experienced officer on the windswept bridge of a ship at sea, the circumstances of C-1 on the night in question were perfectly understandable, and the board appreciated this fact. What was more culpable, however, was the failure of the group to resume its safer, if slower, zigzag course once the main concentration of floating ice was cleared. Obviously, this could not be laid at the door of the senior officer, Commander Byron, who was sound asleep in his sea-cabin, worn out by the all-night vigils of his last days with the convoy. And, given the natural reluctance of junior watch-keeping officers to wake an exhausted senior officer without grave justification, the failure to notify him of the changed circumstances regarding floating ice could hardly come as a surprise.

But, most of all, the officers on the board could sense, throughout their consideration of the facts as reported, the prevalence of an attitude familiar to all the ship's companies of homeward-bound ships nearing journey's end after a long and arduous passage: a condition known, from time immemorial, as "Channel Fever". In anticipation of the safety and comforts of the shore, just hours away, officers and men alike of inward-bound ships tend to disregard the possible dangers and difficulties of the few remaining miles in their eagerness to reach harbour. There was no doubt in the minds of the investigating officers that this attitude, constantly being inveighed against by authority yet always prevalent, was a major factor in the events leading up to *Valleyfield*'s torpedoing and loss, affecting the course and speed being steered, the efficiency of asdic and radar vigilance, and the lookout being maintained from all the bridges in those fateful hours. Indeed, if any one factor could be blamed for *Valleyfield*'s surprising vulnerability on the night in question, it was Channel Fever, pure and simple.

After full consideration of all the factors concerned, no blame could really be assessed against the late Commander Byron for the disposition of his group prior to the torpedoing, however much, with the priceless benefit of hindsight, it might have been wished that he had ordered a resumption of the zigzag and the streaming of CAT gear. An able officer of great experience, killed in action against the enemy, he was not to have his record blemished by officers who understood the circumstances that shaped his decisions.

The board now turned its attention to the events subsequent to *Valleyfield*'s sinking. Here again the record was damning on the face of it: four ships, steaming in close company, had allowed the loss of their senior ship to pass unnoticed for a remarkably long period, had then failed to detect a U-boat obviously in close contact, and had conducted rescue operations in so tardy and ineffective a manner that the greater part of the survivors of the torpedoing, nearly all unhurt when they entered the water, had perished of drowning or exposure. How could such an appalling performance have been put up by an experienced group commanded by capable and efficient officers?

Inevitably, much of the burden of the board's deliberations fell on the shoulders of *Giffard*'s commanding officer, Lieutenant-Commander Charles Petersen. As commanding officer of one of the two ships closest to *Valleyfield* and the first to notice her disappearance, he had assumed temporary command of the leaderless group and, in so doing, had shouldered most of the responsibility for the subsequent conduct of operations.

It was not, it would seem, an impressive record. Despite the fact that his officer of the watch had actually witnessed the torpedoing, and despite the fact that both visual and radar contact had disappeared under good conditions of visibility and radar efficiency, Petersen had been unable to accept the facts of *Valleyfield*'s sinking for an inordinate period of time. His signalman had called her repeatedly by flashing light directed at her last known position without answer, but Petersen had continued to close without making any signal to the remainder of the group. Only when he actually sighted survivors in the water would he accept the fact of *Valleyfield*'s sinking.

Finally, and most damning of all, it was not until well after midnight, half an hour after the torpedoing had been witnessed from his own bridge, that Petersen first informed the other ships in the group that *Valleyfield* had been torpedoed, having already ordered them to close the site.

As Captain Rowland, Captain (D), noted of this crucial delay:

"It is thought that the loss of the senior officer of a group will inevitably produce a certain degree of confusion. On this occasion much valuable time was lost before the situation was appreciated."

In other words, experienced officers could understand, if they could not condone, why Petersen took eighteen vital minutes to make his first signal to the group, and half an hour to tell them what had happened.

But now the circumstances of the real tragedy, the terrible dilemmas that would both claim the lives of scores of *Valleyfield* survivors and permit their enemy to escape unscathed, had to be dealt with. Petersen had been thrust into the classic situation faced by commanders of all escort vessels after sinkings: to rescue survivors as a first priority, or to go after the U-boat responsible?

Sadly, but understandably, faced with the cruel decision, he had dithered. He had delayed too long in hasty, ineffectual rescue attempts, before embarking on a perfunctory, and therefore useless, radar search, a hunt that, however inadequate, occupied so many precious minutes that many of *Valleyfield*'s survivors were to die in the interim. Returning to the scene, he was the victim of yet another classic dilemma involving priorities: which was most important, the preservation of his ship or the rescuing of survivors? In bright moonlight and the known presence of the enemy, he hesitated about lying stopped and vulnerable, yet men were dying by the minute in the freezing water. Again, Petersen had dithered; he had kept way on, in order to point up-moon, while attempting to pull survivors aboard. The advantage he gained was negligible, yet it was won at the cost of lives lost. Some survivors were drawn down by the screw wash; others, including *Valleyfield*'s commanding officer, were unable to be pulled overside because of the momentum of the ship through the water, and were lost.

A careful review of the situation could leave no doubt: much of the staggering loss of life among *Valleyfield*'s survivors had been incurred by *Giffard*'s delay in recognizing that the frigate had been torpedoed, in her decision to delay rescue attempts until she had made a token search for the U-boat responsible, and by keeping the ship under way, albeit very slowly, while attempting to pull helpless men out of the freezing water. Above all, her greatest failure had been in neglecting for so long to inform the other ships in the group; as Commodore Taylor, Flag Officer, Newfoundland, noted: "The commanding officer, HMCS *Giffard*, should have recognized the ships of the group were well placed to order 'Close and carry out Observant anti-clockwise round *Valleyfield* (or my own position)' as soon as he knew that something had happened to HMCS *Valleyfield*. It is considered that in this way there was a very good chance that the U-boat would have been detected by HMCS *Halifax*. It is difficult to understand why, having realized that something had happened at 2343, as shown by his altering course towards *Valleyfield* at that time, the commanding officer, HMCS *Giffard*, made no signal to institute a search for the enemy until 0001, a matter of 18 minutes later."

About the effectiveness of the search itself, made at the cost of so many survivors' lives, the senior officers had no illusions. "The lack of a plot [track chart compiled by a special action team] from *Giffard* gives reason to doubt the efficiency of her short radar search to detect the submarine," commented Captain (D) in his remarks. "It is noted that even *Giffard* would not have reached the area before 0001, and that the other ships had not turned before this time."

In short, the heavy death toll among survivors of the torpedoing and the subsequent failure to detect the U-boat were the direct result of delay and indecision on the part of Lieutenant-

Commander Petersen, the commanding officer of HMCS *Giffard*.

But this terrible indictment would seem so only to those without experience of the war at sea, and of the agonizing decisions that were constantly required to be made by officers often exhausted by fatigue after sleepless nights and sustained stress, decisions based on intuition as much as on necessarily faulty and incomplete information. In particular, experienced officers — and the members of the board were such — could appreciate the delay in realizing that one's senior officer had suddenly been removed from the scene, and the consequent moments of confusion as junior officers attempted to cope with the emergency and the responsibilities so unexpectedly thrust upon them. In the case of Lieutenant-Commander Petersen, he had displayed initiative in assuming direction of affairs once it was realized that the senior ship had been sunk, although the responsibility was technically not his, and was handed over, as soon as convenient to do so, to the commanding officer of HMCS *Edmundston*. Indicative of this understanding of Petersen's natural reluctance to assume responsibility prematurely were the remarks made by Commodore Taylor: "It is thought that the difficulty in quickly appreciating a situation of this kind is pointed up in the case of the torpedoing of HMS *Woodpecker* of E.G.2 [the most successful and experienced of all Second World War escort groups] where the senior officer of the group in HMS *Starling*, 4,000 yards on *Woodpecker*'s starboard beam, was on the bridge when two flares were sighted followed by an explosion and three lesser explosions. The senior officer, E.G.2 remarks: 'I was extremely slow to appreciate what had occurred and it was not until a signal came from *Woodpecker* reporting herself torpedoed that I realised.' "

The plain truth of the matter, apparent to any experienced

seaman, was that Petersen had done the very best he could, after being thrown into a dreadful situation that he was quite unprepared for and that he could not possibly have foreseen. A capable and experienced commanding officer, he had never before been responsible for co-ordinating the operations of a whole group of ships, and his failure to do so as efficiently as a veteran group commander might have done could hardly be held against him. He had been the victim of circumstance, and his hesitation in reacting to a fast-moving sequence of events was understandable.

While the board could not condone Petersen's delays and lapses in the conduct of both search and rescue, it appreciated that the situation had been beyond him, and that he had attempted to cope to the best of his ability; accordingly it did not censure him in its report. The loss both of *Valleyfield* and of so many of her ship's company was attributable to the conjunction of a whole set of unfortunate circumstances, which had to be accepted as a part of naval operations in time of war.

Having completed its investigations, the court of inquiry was dissolved, and the loss of *Valleyfield* passed into history.

Throughout the wartime fleet of the Royal Canadian Navy, the loss of *Valleyfield* was a bombshell, destroying at a stroke the euphoria that had steadily grown as the Allied grip of the Atlantic sea lanes tightened, month by month. The growing assurance of victory had infected all the forces of the free world, and an aura of smug complacency had affected the intensity with which the war at sea was prosecuted. Added to this was a growing sense of immunity from attack which the enormous superiority of Allied seapower had induced; hunting the few U-boats at sea had taken on the air of a sporting endeavour: so many fugitives to be added to the bag as opportunity offered.

The realization that the hunted could still destroy the hunter was a salutary shock to the Canadian escort groups, a reminder of the inherent vulnerability of any ship at sea in wartime, warship or merchantman. Adding to the impact of the news was the fact that *Valleyfield* was the first — and, as it was to prove, the last — Canadian frigate to be sunk by U-boat attack.

But it was when the casualty list was published that the real shock was brought home to the Royal Canadian Navy. How could such an appalling number of men have been lost from a ship steaming in close company with the other ships of her group? How had the U-boat responsible escaped the wrath of her consorts, in good weather and without the distractions of a convoy to protect? Inevitably the talk turned to dark speculations of bungling, and there were ugly rumours of even worse. Wartime censorship, which allowed no details of the operation beyond the barest facts to be made public, added fuel to the conjectures.

The hapless ships of C-1, while conscious that they had not exactly covered themselves with glory, naturally resented the veiled remarks and dark allusions of members of other escort groups, but the aura of suspicion and scandal clung to the incident right up to the end of the war.

For her survivors, *Valleyfield* soon became only a memory, something to be quickly buried under a flood of new ships, new comrades, new experiences. After long survivors' leave, most of them returned to sea in new ships, others to postings in naval establishments ashore. Lieutenants Tate and Warren asked for, and received, a joint posting to the same ship: the new frigate HMCS *Coaticook*, now nearing completion and soon to be commissioned. They went off to join her, Tate still in romantic pursuit of Nursing Sister Stella Davidson, and they enjoyed a happy and uneventful commission through the final months of the war at sea.

After VE day, and the curious "phoney war" that trundled along until the final conclusive victory of VJ day brought an abrupt end to all warlike operations, *Valleyfield*'s survivors were discharged into civilian life to savour the triumph bought so dearly, at the cost of long years of service and hardship and the loss of so many shipmates. Most of them returned, experienced young men, to the homes they had left as boys, to resume the lives so abruptly interrupted as best they could. Some of them married wartime sweethearts — Ian Tate, now plain "Mr.", married a Miss Stella Davidson — and settled down to the business of making a home and a living. For most, the early postwar period was a busy and, despite the difficulties in adjusting from service to civilian life, a happy time, but it was in these bustling postwar years that *Valleyfield* claimed her last casualty.

He was Charles Petersen, commanding officer of HMCS *Giffard*. He had never returned to *Giffard* after leaving her in St. John's on that fateful morning; he had gone off on long leave and, on returning, had been posted in command of the frigate HMCS *St. Stephen*, fitting out on the West Coast. But in truth the promotion to frigate command was a paper one; his naval career, in practical terms, had ended in the *Valleyfield* debacle. He was never again the man he had been; weighed down with the memories of his ordeal, and of its consequences, he had begun the pattern of hard drinking that was to bring him to an early grave. The still-young father of a young family, Charles Petersen died far from the scene of his terrible ordeal.

Of all the many deaths of the *Valleyfield* disaster, this last was perhaps the cruellest.

End of a Navy

"If blood be the price of admiralty,
Lord God, we ha' paid in full."
RUDYARD KIPLING

VALLEYFIELD was not the last loss suffered by the Royal Canadian Navy in the Second World War, nor was she the worst, in terms of lives lost. No other Allied navy had devoted so great a portion of its resources to the crucial Battle of the Atlantic, and the decisive victory in that all-important battle, on which hung the outcome of the war, had been won at a terrible cost in lives and ships. The tiny thirteen-ship pre-war Canadian navy, smallest in the free world, had grown to a wartime sea power at the cost of twenty-four ships sunk and 1,981 officers and men killed in its six-year struggle.

But *Valleyfield*'s loss with so many of her complement had followed on the heels of an even costlier sinking a few days before, rounding out the blackest week in Canada's naval history. On April 29, 1944, HMCS *Athabaskan*, one of the heavily gunned Tribal-class destroyers that were the pride of the fleet, had gone down in a furious running gun-battle with a group of German destroyers off the Ile de Vierge on the northwest coast of France. She had been speedily avenged by her consort, HMCS *Haida*, but her sleek hull, torn by shell and torpedo hits, had slipped beneath the Channel waters, carrying thirteen officers and one hundred and twelve men to their deaths. The "black week" had been the prelude to a black summer, which was to see the losses, all through torpedoing, of the corvettes *Regina* and *Alberni*, at the cost of thirty lives and fifty-nine lives respectively, followed by the sinking of the corvette HMCS *Shawinigan* with every soul aboard, a total of seven officers and eighty-three men. The torpedo sinking of another corvette, HMCS *Trentonian*, with six of her complement, along with that of three Bangor-class minesweepers, *Clayoquot*, *Guysborough*, and *Esquimalt*, at a cost of eight, fifty-one, and forty-four lives respectively, rounded out the ''butcher's bill'' for the closing months of the war with Germany.

It was the torpedoing of the little diesel minesweeper *Esquimalt* in the Halifax approaches during the final days of the war that aroused a deep anger throughout the east-coast naval establishment. It all seemed so stupid, so unnecessary; with Germany's surrender obviously only hours away and with everyone at sea anxious now just to survive, the wiping out of forty-four young lives in the very moment of final victory was almost too cruel to bear.

Everything about the sinking bore the hallmark of a ''Slackers'' operation, complete with the sort of indefinable sloppiness and frustration everyone had come to expect of a Halifax happening. On April 16, 1945, *Esquimalt* had been bumbling along on a sweep of the Halifax approaches on a straight course and with no CAT gear streamed, despite the signalled presence of a U-boat. Off the Sambro light vessel she had stumbled across *U-190*, lying stopped and hoping for a quiet life. Sensing *Esquimalt*'s asdic reflecting from her hull, *U-190* had taken emergency evasive action, firing a torpedo at point-blank range from her stern tube as she turned away. The torpedo hit the little ship on her starboard side, blowing a big hole and killing everyone in the engine room except Stoker Jack Ware, who managed to escape through a hatch in the ship's dummy funnel.

The whaler being flooded, *Esquimalt*'s people got off in four Carley floats, most of them scantily dressed and all of them immersed to some degree in the icy water of the April North Atlantic. Since the ship had sunk almost immediately, no signal had been made; men died in agony, while a few miles away a consort, HMCS *Sarnia*, prowled about the East Halifax lightship all unaware.

Aircraft from Dartmouth flew over the scene minutes after the sinking, mistook the madly waving men on floats for fishermen, and flew on, while yet more men slipped away in silent torment. A couple of minesweepers passed within two miles of the now-desperate survivors without seeing them in the misty morning air, and still men fought for life around the yellow rafts. Some, as they felt life ebbing away, left messages with their comrades, farewells for family or girlfriends. Able Seaman Don White, a Peterborough boy with both arms and legs broken in the explosion, was one such, as was Huntley Fanning of Drumhead, Nova Scotia, a chief electrical artificer who was to have married on his return from this patrol. Some went mad, and died in delirium, jumping from rafts or shouting inanities as death took them. But most clung grimly to life, determined to survive, and their captain, Bob MacMillan, a "wavy-navy" lieutenant who had won a DSC in the Mediterranean, led them in hymns and prayers as the long minutes stretched into hours. When *Sarnia* finally found them, seven hours later, the dead outnumbered the living.

Even now, after the passage of forty years, Canadian naval veterans grow angry when *Esquimalt*'s sinking is recalled. Angry with NSHQ. After more than five years of war, why was *Esquimalt* still carrying Stone Age asdic and a terrible old SW2C set in an era of sophisticated radar? Why were U-boat dispositions being signalled on a frequency neither she nor many other similar ships could monitor? But most of the anger is still directed at German U-boat command. With the Reich collapsing in ruins and surrender terms already being considered; with every man and every ship required to save what was left of the German armies trapped in the Baltic, what was the point of sending *U-190* to operate off Halifax half the world away? What possible benefit could accrue from any ship she might sink there when Germany herself was at her last gasp?

On May 12 *U-190* surrendered to the Canadian corvettes *Thorlock* and *Victoriaville*, and while many Canadian navy men admired the tenacity and strength of purpose of her commander, Edwin Reith, and his worn-out crew, there were many more who felt only a deep anger at what they considered a totally unnecessary sinking, and one that had cost the lives of so many comrades who had survived long years of war only to die on the very threshold of peace.

But these were only the final items on the long casualty list of men and ships lost in the navy's long, uphill battle to win control of the sea from German raiders, submarines, and aircraft. HMCS *Fraser* had been the first of the pre-war destroyers to be sunk, run down by the British cruiser HMS *Calcutta* in a night action in the Bay of Biscay, but she was to be followed by her sister destroyers *Ottawa* and *Margaree*, and then the excruciating loss of HMCS *Skeena*, veteran leader of the famous "Barber-pole Brigade", wrecked on the rocks of Videy Island in a wild Iceland gale.

No loss was felt more keenly throughout the fleet than the sinking, by a new acoustic-torpedo weapon encountered for the first time, of the elderly former U.S. "four-stacker" HMCS *St. Croix*. Victor in many a U-boat encounter, the tough old lady had taken sixty-seven of her complement down with her, and all but one of her eighty-one survivors were drowned when their rescuing ship, the Royal Navy frigate HMS *Itchen*, was sunk immediately afterwards. Only one man, a stoker, was to survive from the old destroyer's complement of one hundred and forty-eight officers and men.

The Royal Canadian Navy paid its dues in warmer seas, too. HMCS *Louisburg*, a corvette, took forty of her ship's company with her when she was hit by an aerial torpedo north of Oran in the Mediterranean, to be followed by another corvette, HMCS *Weyburn*, lost with six officers and two men off Cape Spartel, in the Straits of Gibraltar.

There had been ships lost in the St. Lawrence even before the campaigns of 1942, which had taken *Raccoon* and *Charlottetown*. The little ex-First World War minesweeper HMCS *Bras d'Or* had been lost in a furious gale there, foundering with all hands, and the Bangor HMCS *Chedabucto* was run down by the cable ship *Lord Kelvin*.

But it was the North Atlantic itself which claimed most victims, in ships sunk by torpedo or collision. One of the early corvettes, HMCS *Levis*, had been the navy's first war loss, torpedoed off Greenland with the loss of eighteen lives, and another early ship, HMCS *Windflower*, was run down and sunk by a merchant vessel, an ever-present hazard in the early pre-radar days of convoy escort. Her sister ship, HMCS *Spikenard*, was torpedoed and lost with fifty-seven of her complement halfway between Iceland and Ireland, and the veteran River-class destroyer HMCS *Ottawa* took one hundred and thirteen of her officers and men with her when she was torpedoed in mid-Atlantic.

Yet all this cost — twenty-four ships lost with nearly two thousand officers and men — was merely the price of victory: control of the North Atlantic, across which must pass the men and materials of war which knit the power of the New World to the Old. It was victory, clear and decisive and overwhelming, and one in which the Royal Canadian Navy had played an increasingly dominant role. By the war's end it was a major naval power, and its ships had escorted 25,343 merchantmen carrying 180 million tons of cargo safely to their destinations, had destroyed 23 U-boats, captured 24, and assisted in the killing of many more. It was the most highly specialized anti-submarine navy in the world, and its great fleet of 378 warships and 400 auxiliaries was manned now by war-hardened and experienced officers and men who included some of the leading Allied specialists in their fields of expertise.

With the coming of peace in 1945, this enormous wartime force was, of course, reduced to a fraction of its size, in both ships and men. Yet after the inevitable period of adjustment and alteration, Canada embarked upon the difficult postwar period with a modern, versatile, and well-equipped navy capable of playing its part in the increasingly important role in world affairs that a confident country, in its peacetime euphoria, foresaw for itself. Canada had, after all, emerged from the war as the unquestioned leader of the British Commonwealth dominions, the "special ally" common to both Britain and the United States, and a budding industrial giant untouched by the ravages of war. With Europe in ruins, Japan a smoking devastation, Britain exhausted, and the United States burdened with the daunting task of rebuilding a shattered world, a Canada united by a common wartime experience looked to its navy to express abroad its new-found influence and energy.

In the heady enthusiasm of those early postwar years, the Royal Canadian Navy discharged that role with vigour. It pioneered new technology in anti-submarine detection, a field in which it already excelled, and in the new and developing field of ship-borne helicopter operation. Its small fleet air arm became a byword in NATO circles for its operational skills, and, most significant of all, it led the world in the development of what many naval authorities believed would be the warship of the future: the hydrofoil. Its fabled *Flying 400*, the ship that flew, was the fastest seagoing warship and the largest hydrofoil in the world, and the technology that produced it, stemming from the successful experiments a generation before of F. W. "Casey" Baldwin and Dr. Alexander Bell, was purely Canadian. A happy blend of the innovative and the traditional, Canada's postwar navy had come of age, a force worthy of its wartime sacrifices and of the strong young nation it served so proudly.

Alas, it was not to last. Tensions between older generations and a new "subculture" of youth, fostered and exploited by the entertainment industry, and between an increasingly militant Quebec and the rest of Canada, sapped the confidence of the country. Locked into a Cold War with a swollen Soviet bloc, Youth opted for appeasement, as it had done a generation before. It was now termed unilateral disarmament, but it called, as its predecessor had done, for conciliation rather than confrontation.

Almost overnight, the concept of honourable armed service became unfashionable. A memorial service at the University of Toronto for alumni who had fallen in the Second World War was broken up by a mob of howling, jeering students, and naval veterans attending a dinner at the same city's Royal York Hotel meekly pocketed their medals, many of them decorations for gallantry, rather than confront a derisive crowd of delegates jamming the corridors outside the hall where they were welcoming the new head of their political party, soon to become prime minister.

The confrontation between Canada's French-speaking and English-speaking elements had a disastrous effect on a naval service where the two had always existed side by side with notable amity. Young French Canadians had formed a large proportion of the wartime navy, and a tradition of colourful French-speaking officers, from Victor Brodeur to Louis Audette and Johnny Bernatchez, was a cherished feature of the fleet. Overnight, this easy, amicable association vanished in a cloud of bureaucratic decrees; French-speaking officers and men were shunted into exclusively Francophone ships and departments, regardless of the ensuing difficulties of operating in an English-speaking NATO environment, while French-Canadian ratings and officers were given accelerated promotion and preferred postings in a bureaucratic "catch-up" operation, with the inevitable consequences of anger and resentment on the part of their English-speaking contemporaries.

Like the other armed services, the Royal Canadian Navy suffered heavily from the savage spending cuts inevitable in the prevailing atmosphere of the times. Defence spending was the lowest priority of a series of governments obsessed with social change, and in a remarkably short time the navy was reduced from a potent element of the free world's defences to total insignificance. At a time when Canada's Arctic sovereignty was being called into question for the first time, the navy's ice-breakers were disposed of. As control of the air became essential to control of the sea, Canada's superb fleet air arm was dumped. Its only carrier, after undergoing a complete refit at a scandalously swollen cost, was then scrapped, thus compounding scandal with scandal, and its flyers, ''the finest pilots in the world'', according to a gleeful airline recruiting officer, were forced into civilian life.

The magnificent *Flying 400* hydrofoil, a world leader in the race for the warship of the future, was disposed of to save money, and the navy's last minesweepers were phased out.

A great freeze descended on every aspect of naval operations, and no new construction, rebuilding, or rearming was undertaken. A sort of paralysis held the service in its grip; the navy was dying, and everyone in the service could sense it, and see the portents of its doom on every side: aging ships, dwindling personnel, eroding morale. In 1965 the fleet was down to sixty-five ships; by 1984 it had shrunk to only thirty-eight.

It was not the loss of her war-built fleet, or its crews, that was the Canadian tragedy; ships can always, must always, be replaced. Rather, it was the loss of the traditions and standards, so hardly won and paid for in the cruel wartime years; the mystique that embodies a navy's soul, and transmits from one generation to the next the unique spirit and inspiration that are the essential heart of a fighting service. In a remarkably short time Canada gave away its hard-won status as a world sea power and abandoned its role as a major defender of western freedom. Few Canadians seemed aware of the loss, and fewer still seemed to care.

More than anything else, it was a sort of xenophobia, arising out of a shallow but fervid new nationalism whipped up in Ottawa, that devastated Canada's navy. In a drive to eliminate any vestige, however slight, of links with Britain that might smack of colonialism, the navy was stripped of its admirals, its ensign, its uniform, its traditions, its name.

It would be difficult to say which of these losses was the

most devastating. The enforced resignation of its high-level officers deprived the service of the benefit of senior wartime experience, a treasure beyond price in an increasingly peacetime force. The dropping of the white ensign, aesthetically the most beautiful of all service standards, meant the loss not only of the morale-boosting identification with victorious traditions stretching back through the centuries, but also of membership in the British Commonwealth white-ensign club, a cosy naval family spread around the world.

Perhaps, though, it was the loss of the traditional navy-blue uniform that, more than any other measure, brought home to veteran sailors the full dimensions of the disaster that had engulfed their service. There is a very real fraternity of the sea, common to the men of all nations, all navies, engendered by the sharing of common dangers, and the badge of that fraternity is the navy-blue uniform worn by all the world's navies. With the adoption of drab olive-green clothing, Canada became odd man out, her sailors the object of derision in the naval ports of the world.

Having finally throttled the navy, the federal government now danced on its grave. The very word "navy" was to be abolished: henceforth the service — what was left of it — was to be called "Marcom", which is bureaucratic jargon for "Maritime Command". "Navy", a fine old four-letter word, simple and descriptive and everywhere understood, was scrapped in favour of mere jargon, a word not to be found in any dictionary. There was more to follow: the whole spectrum of naval rank and ratings was to be rooted out and replaced with mere verbal garbage, so that a signalman, for example, was to be known as a "Visual Communicator", and ships could be commanded by Lieutenant-Colonels rather than Commanders.

It was the end; the end of a proud service that had served

Canada well through two world wars, but it is perhaps fair to say that the Ottawa bureaucrats who had destroyed it were unaware of the full extent of what they had done. To the civilian mind, the alterations may have appeared as merely cosmetic: a few changes in flag and uniform, in nomenclature and rank structure. Pay and allowances were untouched, the men would be well clothed and fed; what was there to get excited about?

What was overlooked, of course, was the curious fact that, in a fighting service, men are notoriously reluctant to risk their lives for sensible civilian motives—pay, position, or perks—yet will cheerfully die in defence of mere intangibles. Men fight, and die, for pride, not patriotism or money, and pride is engendered in symbols, in little, inconsequential things, flags and uniforms and traditions that set them apart from other men. In the waterborne appendage to a universal service that was "Marcom", there was nothing to engender *esprit de corps*; stripped of its ensign, its uniform, its ranks, ratings, and name, the service was dead, and its men, like its few aging ships, mouldered in neglect, unheeded by a nation caught up in the heady euphoria of the "Swinging Sixties", and the "Sexy Seventies", as headline-writers hailed each decade, and by a government concerned with "rights", rather than responsibilities.

Reveille

THE REAL LEGACY of Canada's war at sea, especially of the Triangle Run, the Gulf war, and the endless patrols of home waters, was an awareness of the country's vulnerability from the sea. For all their enormous coastline, Canadians had always regarded themselves as a continental nation, more concerned with matters of the land than of the sea. But the generation of us who came of age in the armed yachts, the motor launches, the Bangors and corvettes and destroyers of the Second World War, stepped from the sheltered comfort of our inland homes into the harsh realities of a maritime world, and the transition would shape our outlook and change our values for ever.

We learned that, in the real world, might counts for more than right; that ultimately, for all the pretensions and posturing of politicians, the great issues of the world are determined by force. Freedom, we learned, survived not on its own merits, but only when it was defended against tyranny by superior force. If you were not prepared to die for your system, you must accept the system of an enemy who was prepared to die for his.

Under the terrible testing of the elements and an unseen enemy, a whole new set of standards emerged, far different from those we had accepted in the comfortable world of peace. We learned to value character above intellect, courage above cleverness, and, huddled in the craven cowardice common to all normal men, we learned to esteem bravery as the rarest and noblest of human virtues. We learned, the hard way, that discipline is what wins wars, triumphing over mere numbers, intelligence, or courage, and that pride would keep us going long after patriotism flagged.

But, above all, we learned to accept the world as it really is, a world in which conflict is an integral and, indeed, an indispensable part of the scheme of things, the essential element in the evolution and natural balance of all living things. We longed for peace, for the comfort and security it would bring, but all of us recognized it for what it was: a mere cessation of the conflict natural to life on this planet, a fragile state to be prolonged and preserved only by constant effort, maintained by defences strong enough to deter violence, external or domestic.

But the Canada we came back to, and in which we have learned to live and make our way after often painful adjustment, became a country which seemed to believe that good intentions were all, that "wishing would make it so", that anything unpleasant, be it war or poverty or hatred, could simply be legislated out of existence. In the face of the whole record of human existence, thousands upon thousands of years of endless conflict, we were to believe that armed defence forces were obsolete in a world governed by reason, where the most fundamental difference between nations could be resolved by a good talk.

It is only recently that this comfortable concept of the world about us has been changing. It was awkward to learn, for example, that Soviet nuclear submarines regularly used Arctic waters which we claimed, but where we could not go, and that in a wartime emergency Russia planned to convert them to "armed bastions" by laying mines, which we cannot sweep, in "our" northwest passage to seal off interference by U.S. submarines. When Toronto and Winnipeg and the whole industrial area between lie within easy reach of such submarines' missiles, it is only natural to consider the advantage of reviving a navy of some sort. Canada has begun to learn again the lesson brought home so effectively by the U-boat intrusions into the St. Lawrence over forty years ago; we are a maritime nation, like it or not, and we must learn to act accordingly. It is from the sea that our greatest menace comes, and it is on the sea that we must build our defences.

The reawakening of interest in Canada's naval affairs coincided with, and perhaps even stemmed from, a remarkable encounter in London, England. At a reception for visiting Canadian veterans at Canada House, the Canadian High Commissioner, shaking hands with one of a long line of war veterans filing past him, gave a start and exclaimed, "My God, is it you, Yeo?"

The High Commissioner was Jake Warren, formerly *Valleyfield*'s navigating officer; the visiting veteran was Irving Kaplan, formerly signal yeoman aboard *Valleyfield*, and they had not seen or heard of each other since they had last parted in the naval hospital at St. John's over thirty-five years before. From this chance encounter came a remarkable gathering of *Valleyfield* survivors; on May 7, 1981, thirty-seven years to the day after their frigate had sunk, seventeen former *Valleyfield* men met in an Ottawa hotel suite for a moving and emotional reunion, a group of middle-aged veterans recalling the terrible circumstances that had parted them, as young men, long before, and describing briefly what had befallen them since.

The reunion naturally attracted a good deal of media coverage, and accordingly a circumstance of that gathering received widespread attention. An attempt to find a bugler to sound the Last Post at a wreath-laying ceremony at the national war memorial brought home to *Valleyfield* veterans, and to a watching national television and newspaper audience, the startling fact that in the nation's capital there was not a single naval bugler left. The figure in traditional navy blues who sounded the bugle calls at the stirring ceremony was a sea cadet, and perhaps more than anything else this emphasized to Canadians across the country the shocking demise of their once-proud navy.

In the intervening years, a reawakening interest in the parlous state of Canada's defences generally and of its maritime force in particular has brought about some dramatic changes. To begin with, the term "navy" began to reappear, not only in newspapers but in Ottawa corridors, in place of the hated "Marcom". And the navy was even to have some new ships to replace a few, at least, of its obsolete fleet, and its officers and men were again to be dressed in traditional navy blue, rather than the detested service-station green. Little by little, Canada's navy was being reborn, and not a moment too soon.

It had never entirely disappeared. Although the *Stadacona* officers' mess in Halifax had been moved into a new building, as bland and banal as a shopping plaza, Admiralty House was left in its Georgian elegance to house a naval museum, loaded with the artifacts of more than a century of naval history and thronged with a thousand ghosts. Near by in the Battle of the Atlantic chapel, built with donations from Canada's naval veterans, Russell Goodman's magnificent front window, a masterpiece in stained glass, and a Garden of Remembrance with ships' name plaques among the roses, preserve the memory of the navy's war dead.

Nobody today would dream of calling Canada's newest provincial capital city "Newfyjohn", but tucked away in the heart of downtown St. John's is a living survival of the city's glory days as a famous wartime naval base. The Crowsnest, the old Seagoing Officers Club, lives on today as a private club. It has an easier side entrance now, replacing the "fifty-nine steps" notorious throughout the Atlantic escort groups of the Second World War, but its walls are still lined with the colourful crests of the ships from the mid-ocean and Triangle runs, and its firelit ambience is redolent of the days when it was packed nightly with cheerful young men from the corvette navy.

But the most remarkable reminder of that wartime navy is to be found today at the Maritime Museum on the Halifax waterfront. HMCS *Sackville*, the last corvette and the only survivor of the largest class of warships ever built, lies alongside in all the spectacular splendour of her Western Approaches camouflage, restored to her wartime configuration, from the ancient four-inch gun on her fo'c'sle to the depth-charge traps and throwers aft.

Yacht-like in her white and pastel paint, she is a striking contrast to the drab greys of today's warships, and her flare and sheer and air of cocky purpose will bring a gleam — and a tear — to the eye of every wartime sailor who catches sight of her. Like *Victory* in England or *Old Ironsides* in the United States, she is the embodiment of an era of national greatness, when Canada came of age and took her rightful place among the maritime powers of the free world.

More than anything else, this last corvette symbolizes the spirit of Canada in its hour of greatest testing, the very essence of the wartime Royal Canadian Navy. That it should be restored and preserved by the voluntary donations of thousands of individual Canadians is clearest proof that Canada's navy shall never die.

As a parliamentary democracy which embodies its national being in a constitutional monarch, not in some jumped-up partisan politician, Canada has the right to dignify its national institutions as ''royal''. The awakening national interest in our maritime future may well prompt the rebirth of the Royal Canadian Navy, and restoration of the glorious heritage laid up for it by the courage and hardihood of thousands of young men a generation ago, who fought for it and died for it so proudly, both in distant seas and in home waters.

BIBLIOGRAPHY

Broome, Jack. *Make a Signal!* London, Eng.: Putnam, 1955.

Bruce, Harry. *Lifeline: The Story of the Atlantic Ferries and Coastal Boats,* Toronto: Macmillan, 1977.

Essex, James. *Victory on the St. Lawrence; Gaspé and Quebec and the Nazi Submarines*, Erin, Ont.: Boston Mills Press, 1983.

Hadley, Michael. *U-Boats Against Canada: German Submarines in Canadian Waters*. Kingston and Montreal: McGill-Queen's University Press, 1985.

Lawrence, Hal. *A Bloody War: One Man's Memories of the Canadian Navy, 1939-45*. Toronto: Macmillan, 1979.

Lynch, Thomas. *Canada's Flowers: History of the Corvettes of Canada, 1939-1945*. Halifax, N.S.: Nimbus, 1982.

McKee, Fraser. *The Armed Yachts of Canada*. Erin, Ont.: Boston Mills Press, 1983.

Macpherson, Ken, and Burgess, John. *The Ships of Canada's Naval Forces, 1910-1981*. Don Mills, Ont.: Collins, 1981.

Milner, Marc. *North Atlantic Run: The Royal Canadian Navy and the Battle for the Convoys.* Toronto: University of Toronto Press, 1985.

Schull, Joseph. *The Far Distant Ships: An Official Account of Canadian Naval Operations in the Second World War*. Ottawa: Queen's Printer, 1961.

Young, George. *The Short Triangle*. Lunenberg, N.S.: Lunenburg County Press, 1975.